A GALLERY OF PAINTINGS BY CLARK HULINGS

A GALLERY OF PAINTINGS BY CLARK HULINGS

WHITE BURRO PUBLISHING

Many people have helped me with this book.

Some have read it and made valuable suggestions.

Others have given special time and energy to
the mechanics of its production.

All have provided enthusiasm and moral support and I am deeply grateful.
They are: Glenn Bradley, Robert Preato, Wayne Wolfe, Charles Winston, Joe Vergara,
Sue Ottinger, Elizabeth Hulings, Lois Brooks, Kate Walsh, Tony Trapani,
Tony Amendola and Billy Mousigian.

But the book would not exist without the special contributions
of skill and energy and *unlimited* patience of Haig Tashjian,
Lois Wagner, Walter Brooks and my wife Mary.

CLARK HULINGS

A Gallery of Paintings by Clark Hulings
First Edition

Copyright © 1986 by Clark Hulings

All rights reserved. Except for use in a review, no part of this book may be
reproduced or used in any way without the written permission of the publisher.

First published in the United States by White Burro Corporation.

Library of Congress Card #85-051223
ISBN 0-9615368-0-2

Editor—Joseph Vergara
Designer—Walter Brooks
Printer—Sterling Regal Inc.
Binder—A. Horowitz & Son

CONTENTS

DEDICATION   VII

INTRODUCTION   IX

LIST OF PLATES   XII

BIOGRAPHY

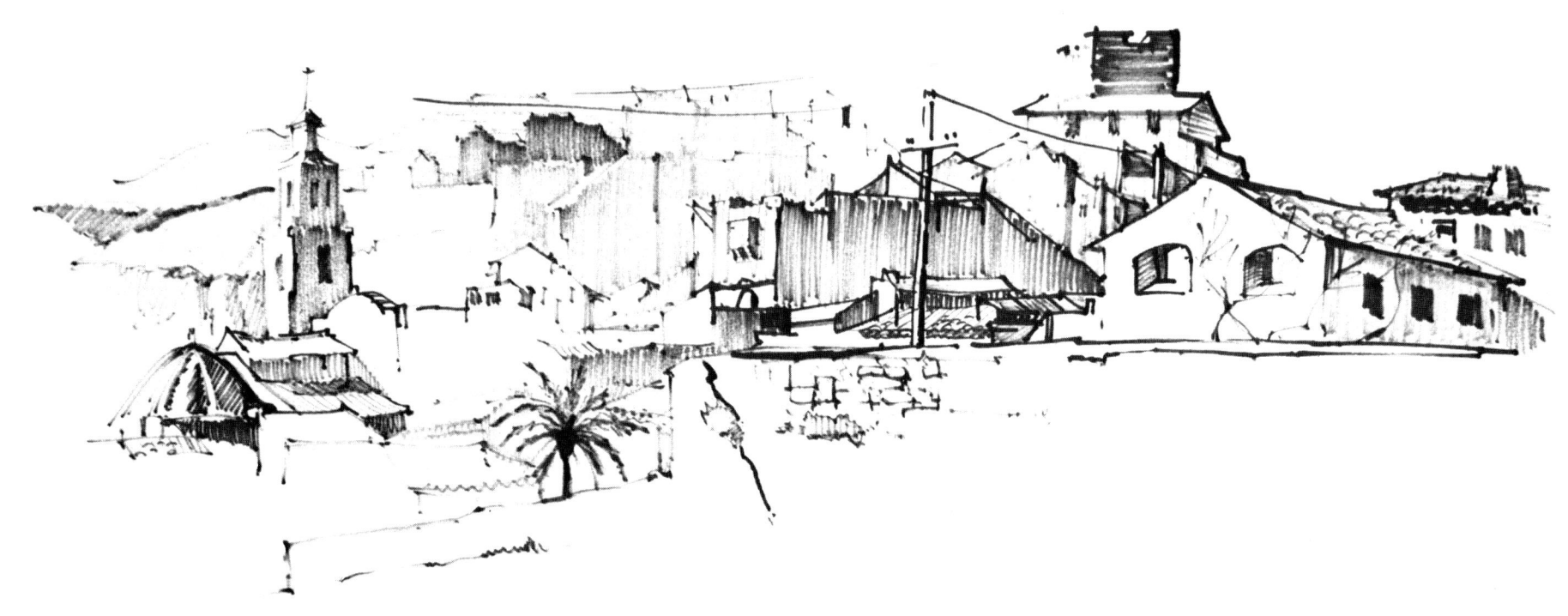

COURTLAND M. HULINGS by CLARK HULINGS

To my father.
It was he who first recognized
whatever talent I possess and he nurtured it.
In the beginning, he found a good teacher for me.
Later, he supported me and encouraged me
in a difficult and uncertain career.
But most of all, he transmitted
his great love of paintings to me.

VIII

INTRODUCTION

Spread out on a giant lightbox in my studio were more than 100 transparencies of my paintings which I had selected as groundwork for this book. Early portraits of subjects long forgotten lay next to recent paintings of the Grand Canyon. There were market scenes, farm scenes, street scenes, country scenes. As I let my eyes range over them, I gradually realized that before me lay virtually my entire life's work. Here was a tangible record of my total creative output, the net result of years spent trying to capture on canvas fleeting scenes of people, places and events that I found memorable and worth preserving.

Studying the transparencies, I asked myself what common threads in style and subject matter ran through these paintings. Did I favor a certain palette of colors, a particular arrangement in my composition? And I wondered what influences in my life had shaped my attitudes and my approach to painting.

I remembered the paintings that hung on the walls of our home when I was a child. They were landscapes and street scenes, mostly Spanish, which my father had collected during his travels. Although he had no inclination to be an artist himself, he loved painting and was an avid museum visitor. We lived then in a suburb of New York City and made occasional trips to the Metropolitan Museum of Art where we naturally headed to his favorites— the realist and impressionist painters.

When I was fourteen, my father's maiden aunt, who lived in New York, had a stroke and it became his custom to look in on her every Saturday. I was taken along for company, at first reluctantly but later eagerly when it was decided that I could visit the Metropolitan Museum while they were together. Soon I had favorite paintings of my own and included them in my weekly rounds. To this day these paintings are still my favorites at the Metropolitan: *Peace and Plenty* by George Innes, *The Wyndham Sisters* by Sargent, *Madame Charpentier and Her Children* by Renoir, *The Noble Slav* by Rembrandt, *Young Woman With a Water Jug* by Vermeer, *The Horse Fair* by Rosa Bonheur, *View of Toledo* by El Greco, *The*

J. Gomez

Guitaras

J. Gomez

Calmady Children by Sir Thomas Lawrence, and *The Rehearsal on the Stage* by Degas.

Sometimes we would have time to go to a gallery or two. I especially liked the Grand Central Art Galleries, where I could enjoy seeing Frieseke's garden portraits of women, Pushman's mysterious Oriental still lifes, and Leigh's western scenes—particularly his sketches of donkeys.

I bought postcards at the museum and a paint set at a hardware store and copied Lawrence's *The Calmady Children*. In one so young and without training, such an ambition must have seemed ridiculous. But nobody laughed. Instead, my father searched for an art teacher and discovered that a master painter, Sigismund Ivanowski, lived right in our town, Westfield, New Jersey. Father showed him my "Calmady Children." Ivanowski agreed to take me as a pupil and I began studying with him on weekends.

Ivanowski was thoroughly trained in the realistic style of the Leningrad Academy at the turn of the century. He taught by inspiration and example. He held class only in the morning because afternoons were spent on his own work—sometimes a landscape, but usually a commissioned portrait. We students were allowed to follow the progress of these paintings. He was much more than just a master of draftsmanship. I once watched him do a wonderfully accurate pen-and-ink drawing from his imagination. The subject was a coach-in-four in full trot as seen from a second-story window—an extraordinary accomplishment. Another time I stood by as he gradually applied glazes, day after day, to the background around a portrait figure. These glazes produced such a feeling of third dimension that you wanted to place your hand in the painting behind the subject's head to check whether the illusion was real.

I was fortunate to be under Ivanowski's tutelage at an early age. Teenagers learn by imitating examples that inspire them. This is as true in painting as it is in sports. Explanations and analyses are for adults.

After three years with Ivanowski, I was threatened with tuberculosis, a disease which had killed my mother. It was decided that I should stay at home rather than face the rigors of freshman college. I was strong enough, however, to study painting with Ivanowski every morning and drawing with George Bridgman in New York every afternoon—provided that I spent twelve hours a night in bed. This program continued for a year.

Later I studied intensively with another great teacher, Frank Reilly, at the Art Students' League. He was a genius at organizing the technical aspects of drawing, painting and composition. He had been a pupil of George Bridgman and Frank Vincent Dumond and had managed to distill their great knowledge into a cohesive, teachable system. He broke every technique down into simple rules which helped us to master the basic mechanical skills quickly. His boundless energy and enthusiasm carried us along and brought out our best efforts. His no-nonsense approach was an ideal complement to the poetic osmosis of Ivanowski's teaching. They are both with me every day in my memory, whispering admonitions and continuing to shape and influence my painting style.

To these inspirational mentors, I must add the great magazine illustrators. My formative years luckily came during the golden age of illustration, before television killed it. Every week I looked forward to spending my allowance on story magazines so I could feast on the pictures made by Dean Cornwell, Harold Von Schmidt and Norman Rockwell. Their styles were lively, energetic and wonderful, and I wanted to emulate them.

Norman Rockwell was special. I had seen original examples of his work when I was seventeen—an exhibition of paintings to illustrate editions of *Tom Sawyer* and *Huckleberry Finn*. His understanding of light, texture and shape must surely rank him with the great painters.

As I studied the pictures on my lightbox, I could see clearly how much my painting style owes to my teachers and my painter idols. Even so, I have never felt inclined to copy the subject matter of these titans. While the development of my style was an ongoing thing, honed over many years, my tendency to continue painting the same motifs again and again seems to be locked into place by nostalgia. A reader casually leafing through this collection must notice that the subject matter is heavily weighted toward Spain and Mexico, with their marketplaces and burros.

When I was an infant and my sister was two, our mother died and we went to live with our maternal grandparents. The house included three uncles and an aunt, all eager to envelop us with love and attention. Our father, an engineer, was sent by his firm to Spain where, after a time, he married the daughter of the British consul. By the time I was four, they had formed a settled household and wanted my sister and me with them. So we were whisked away by two strangers to a foreign land and placed in the hands of an English governess and a Spanish maid. I can remember having my afternoon lessons with Miss Camp at the lunch table. I learned to count and cipher with the grains of rice that remained to be eaten.

The strict routine of our days was mercifully relieved from time to time by our maid, Maria. Rather than take us to the park to play with the little English children as she had been instructed, she would take us instead to her parents' home, a sort of Spanish version of the warm household we had left in America. It boasted a donkey, some chickens and some goats. Other times we went to El Mercado Central, or Central Market, where Maria's boyfriend worked. We became the mascots of the stallkeepers, and their goods became our playthings. The colors, the smells, the noise, the excitement and the attention paid to us made it a wonderful playground. The English children in the park playground could not compete. We were Maria's willing conspirators.

Weekends were special because we spent them with our father and our new mother. Often we would go to the beach to swim or we would take the dusty auto trip to Buñol for a picnic. I can remember the olive and ochre landscape well—the distant mountains, the nearby hills laced with tunnels and a toylike train disappearing and reappearing as it snaked its way across the scene.

If it is nostalgia that induces me to paint markets and donkeys and Spanish landscapes, things which were part of my distant childhood, perhaps it is also nostalgia that moves me to search out rustic places with bygone lifestyles.

For an artist who likes to study and paint what he can see rather than what he can imagine, modernism presents a problem. If he likes to paint farms being worked with animals instead of tractors, if he likes to paint old buildings, dirt roads and wooden fences instead of concrete block buildings, macadam roads and cyclone wire fences, then he must go to a place where life remains simple and more primitive.

But my rustic world is fast shrinking. The open-air markets are giving way to supermarkets. No more wooden stalls sheltered by colorful canvas awnings—no more donkey "parking lots"—no more donkeys!

The plan of my book may appear haphazard, and so be it. There is some slight concession to order with occasional loose groupings of paintings by subject matter, chronology or geography. But in general each painting shown, with its own little essay or anecdote, is independent of the others. The arrangement, such as it is, stems from my own stream of consciousness.

CLARK HULINGS

LIST OF PLATES

Plate 1. EL MERCADO CENTRAL—Valencia
Plate 2. EL MERCADO CENTRAL—Valencia (detail)
Plate 3. THE SCAVENGERS
Plate 4. RESTAURANTE VICENTE—Saler
Plate 5. RESTAURANTE VICENTE—(detail)
Plate 6. THE RED RAINCOAT—Valencia
Plate 7. ILE DE LA CITÉ—Paris
Plate 8. OLD LADY IN BLACK
Plate 9. CONVERSATION
Plate 10. ONTENIENTE
Plate 11. ONTENIENTE (detail)
Plate 12. GRANADA PRODUCE STALL
Plate 13. GRANADA PLAZA
Plate 14. MULES OF TARANCÓN, STANDING
Plate 15. MULES OF TARANCÓN, RUNNING
Plate 16. TORREMOLINOS AT DAWN
Plate 17. CASA SUECIA (Swedish House)
Plate 18. ALTEA (detail–girl)
Plate 19. ALTEA
Plate 20. ALTEA (detail–wall)
Plate 21. THE GIRL AND THE CAT
Plate 22. FAMILY PORTRAIT
Plate 23. THAT GREEK TREE PICTURE
Plate 24. GREEK WOMEN WASHING
Plate 25. WHITE ROSES WITH ONION
Plate 26. BACKLIT ROSE
Plate 27. CHRYSANTHEMUMS
Plate 28. THE SPIRIT LAMP
Plate 29. STILL LIFE WITH VIOLETS
Plate 30. MARY, ELIZABETH AND PAULINE
Plate 31. ELIZABETH, BABY
Plate 32. ELIZABETH, 1½ YEARS
Plate 33. ELIZABETH AND FEATHER, 8 YEARS
Plate 34. ELIZABETH, 12 YEARS
Plate 35. THE SPANISH SHAWL DRAWING
Plate 36. SAN JOŚE MISSION—San Antonio
Plate 37. WATERCOLOR ROSES
Plate 38. CHURCH AT TRAMPAS—New Mexico
Plate 39. INDIAN MARKET
Plate 40. MAN OF PLAV
Plate 41. EGYPTIANS
Plate 42. KONYA MOSQUE
Plate 43. CHURCH—Rieka, Yugoslavia
Plate 44. PARIS VIGNETTE
Plate 45. YUGOSLAVIAN STREET PHOTOGRAPHER
Plate 46. LITTLE CHAPEL AT DUBROVNIK
Plate 47. DUBROVNIK CATHEDRAL
Plate 48. MARKET SCENE I—Skopje
Plate 49. MARKET SCENE II—Skopje
Plate 50. OUTSKIRTS OF THE SKOPJE MARKET
Plate 51. COVERED POOL—Istanbul
Plate 52. CARRIAGE TAXI—Konya, Turkey
Plate 53. QUARRY CART—Mersin, Turkey
Plate 54. TEMPLE OF KARNAK—Luxor
Plate 55. LUXOR FERRYBOAT
Plate 56. CAIRO RUG MERCHANT
Plate 57. THE LONELY MAN
Plate 58. RAINY STREET—Sicily
Plate 59. RANDAZZO—Sicily
Plate 60. STREET IN NAPLES
Plate 61. SUZY
Plate 62. NANCY
Plate 63. SARA
Plate 64. SYLVIA
Plate 65. A ROOFTOP VIEW OF ARGENTAT
Plate 66. FEEDING THE CHICKENS
Plate 67. VILLE FRANCHE
Plate 68. THE RED SWING—Brantôme
Plate 69. HIERSAC CHÂTEAU
Plate 70. HIERSAC CHÂTEAU—(sketch, first visit)
Plate 71. HIERSAC CHÂTEAU—(sketch, second visit)
Plate 72. CLOTH VENDORS—San Miguel de Allende
Plate 73. THE PINK SERAPE
Plate 74. THE LOWER MARKET
Plate 75. KALEIDOSCOPE
Plate 76. KALEIDOSCOPE (detail–figures)
Plate 77. KALEIDOSCOPE (detail–head)

Plate 78. THE MEXICAN ROSARY MAN
Plate 79. WINDY MARKET DAY
Plate 80. THE MELON STAND
Plate 81. CHAPALA FRUIT VENDOR
Plate 82. THE GUARDIAN
Plate 83. BURRO ALLEY, SANTA FE, 1900
Plate 84. ASINO ALLEY
Plate 85. SAN MIGUEL WOOD MERCHANT
Plate 86. CHICHICASTENANGO—Guatemala
Plate 87. THE PINK PARASOL
Plate 88. THE PLASTIC BAG LADY
Plate 89. AFTERNOON BUS
Plate 90. VELEZ MÁLAGA COURTYARD
Plate 91. SALTILLO—Mexico
Plate 92. TIMELESS ADOBE (sketch)
Plate 93. TIMELESS ADOBE
Plate 94. WOODBEARERS OF CHIMAYO
Plate 95. LOUISIANA CABIN
Plate 96. TAXCO HORSEMAN
Plate 97. MÁLAGA BARRIO
Plate 98. NOONDAY, ANDALUSIA
Plate 99. WOMEN WASHING—Comonfort, Mexico
Plate 100. HOT SPRINGS
Plate 101. MULE IN THE RAIN
Plate 102. THE CANDLE SELLER
Plate 103. LA GRANJA
Plate 104. HEXAGONAL BARNS
Plate 105. BELOW RONDA
Plate 106. THE CHAIRMAKER
Plate 107. WASHERWOMAN ON THE ROOF
Plate 108. LA ABUELA
Plate 109. THE YELLOW BEDSPREAD
Plate 110. THE GREEN WATERING CAN
Plate 111. THE OLIVE GROVE
Plate 112. A STUDY IN EARLY MORNING LIGHT
Plate 113. NOONDAY SUN
Plate 114. ÚBEDA AT DUSK
Plate 115. EL GRAO
Plate 116. OFF PALACE AVENUE
Plate 117. JOSÉ ANTONIO VARGAS
Plate 118. CUYAMUNGUE
Plate 119. BROKEN COTTONWOODS—Taos
Plate 120. NOVEMBER SUNLIGHT—Nambe, New Mexico
Plate 121. LOWER COLONIAS
Plate 122. RODRIGUEZ STREET
Plate 123. KAIBAB TRAIL, FALL
Plate 124. KAIBAB TRAIL, WINTER
Plate 125. BRIGHT ANGEL TRAIL
Plate 126. PACK TRAIN
Plate 127. THE GRAY BARN
Plate 128. WASHINGTON MEADOW
Plate 129. THE ACOMA POTTER
Plate 130. THE KACHINA DOLL MAKER
Plate 131. THE KACHINA DOLL MAKER (sketch)
Plate 132. THE JUNGFRAU
Plate 133. CERISE
Plate 134. GIRL WATERING HER BURRO
Plate 135. AFTON VILLA
Plate 136. GREENWOOD
Plate 137. SPANISH MOSS GATHERER
Plate 138. PIERRE PART
Plate 139. WINDRUSH PLANTATION COTTAGE
Plate 140. LOUISIANA FISHERWOMAN
Plate 141. OLD MANOR HOUSE BY THE SEA
Plate 142. THATCH DELIVERY
Plate 143. EMPTY CART
Plate 144. EMPTY CART (detail)
Plate 145. BEFORE THE IRISH WIND
Plate 146. VAL CONEELEY'S HOUSE (sketch)
Plate 147. BURRO PULLING LOGS AT ASWAN
Plate 148. OLD MAN GOING HOME
Plate 149. FLOWER BURRO
Plate 150. BOY FILLING WATER CANS
Plate 151. BOY LEADING WATER BURRO
Plate 152. SANTA FE FESTIVAL POSTER BURRO
Plate 153. TWO BURROS IN AN ALLEY
Plate 154. THE BABY SITTER
Plate 155. BROWN MULE

Plate 1. EL MERCADO CENTRAL—Valencia

This is the market where my sister and I were taken as small children. Years later, when I returned to Valencia, the market looked just as I remembered it. But viewed through adult eyes, it was even grander than the picture I had carried in my head. I was particularly struck by the beauty of the special diffused light; it was almost churchlike. The market was built in the days when craftsmanship was prized. Even the windows of the building boast delicate wrought-iron designs.

The market bustled with activity, offering unlimited opportunities for composition. There was a wide variety of human subject matter in interesting poses as people stopped to examine the displayed merchandise or to pass a few words with friends and shopkeepers. There were vegetables, kitchenware, fruit, fish, chickens, fabrics, ceramics—an almost infinite inventory of shapes, colors and textures constantly shifting and changing with the play of light and movement of the crowds.

The market is old and remains the same. But here and there a jarring note appears: a pile of plastic toys and pails, a few plastic awnings, aluminum spotlights, an occasional fluorescent light.

All in all, I like to visit markets best after they have closed. Then only a few people remain. Some of the stalls are covered, awaiting the next day. Sometimes the tile floor is hosed down and sparkles with reflections. A lone man is sweeping up refuse. An old lady in black scavenges for a few pieces of bruised fruit or a fish that accidentally slipped to the floor.

Plate 2. EL MERCADO CENTRAL—Valencia (detail)

These two scavengers standing outside the Mercado Central in Valencia have retrieved an illustrated weekly magazine and they're looking through it. One of them has found something sensational and is reading it aloud to the other.

The picture brings to mind some feelings I have about the constructive use of the camera and about selecting poses. Most accomplished artists have enough experience and ability to draw figures out of their heads. They can produce anatomically correct, well-draped, well-drawn figures. But when one draws from his own knowledge he is depending on a limited resource and runs the risk of repeating himself, of giving a sameness to his work. If, on the other hand, he paints from a variety of images supplied by his camera, he will produce work that has originality and life.

These two ladies were standing there for several minutes and I took perhaps fifteen or twenty photographs of them. Their shoulders leaned a certain way. They stood first on one foot and then the other. They fussed with their shopping sacks. I finished with a fine collection of subtle poses. Had the women been in animated conversation, there would have been an even greater variety of gesture. People talk with their hands. They shift burdens from one arm to the other. Perhaps a child is holding onto one hand, making some little movement the way children do, twisting a leg or trying to pull away. Human beings do things in a natural way that simply can't be imagined.

The artist using a camera must, of course, learn to select and interpret the poses which best serve his purpose.

Viewing my choice for the two scavengers, I realize that I have unconsciously heeded a rule put down to me years ago by my teacher Ivanowski. He said: "Always oppose tension with relaxation—the active with the passive. This applies to all things with the possibility of movement." He mentioned this while helping me to pose my mother for a portrait. He seated her with one hand clutching the arm of the chair and the other lying limp in her lap.

Here you can see from the hunch of her shoulders that the woman on the left is busy reading, while the other woman is listening—passive.

Plate 3. THE SCAVENGERS

Plate 4. RESTAURANTE VICENTE—Saler

This painting is in our living room and we call it "the old car picture." The tiny village of Saler is along the shore of the Mediterranean near the port serving Valencia. When I was a child, we often went there to swim and would have our breakfast at the Restaurante Vicente before crossing the street and walking through the pine-covered sand dunes to the beach.

Some thirty years later on a nostalgic tour of Spain I visited Valencia and its environs and found Saler still there—pine trees, *panadería*, and the Restaurante Vicente. In front was the old black car with the bamboo fishing pole slung over the roof, reminiscent of some other old black car in my memory.

Only the wide-windowed apartment house under construction next door, the little Seat auto, the aluminum pipe chairs, and the Pepsi Cola sign testified to Saler's recent leap into the modern world and presaged what was to come later. The old black car actually had only two doors and was considerably shorter than the one you see here. As the painting developed it became evident that the composition required a dark shape larger than the original car provided. This need was met by stretching the car out and adding back doors. The altered car always puzzled an automobile advertising artist friend of ours who prided himself on his familiarity with every old model.

What came later in the development of taste and modernism was evident on still another visit twenty years later. The entire scene—the Restaurante Vicente, the bakery, walls, doors, windows, tables, chairs, even faded awnings—had been painted shiny aluminum. Only the old Pepsi Cola sign had escaped the brush.

Plate 5. RESTAURANTE VICENTE—(detail)

Plate 6. THE RED RAINCOAT—Valencia

As I struggle to write about my paintings I gain more and more respect for professional writers. I have tried several times to write poetically about flower markets and failed. So, leaving those attempts for another time, I offer here simply a few notes of advice to myself.

Use strong undiluted color very sparingly. An effect of richness can be produced only with grayed-down color discreetly highlighted with small areas of pure color from the tube. Too much strong color looks garish, not rich.

Separate color areas with buffers of gray. This, too, will ensure richness. The gray or black lead between colors in stained glass serves this purpose—that's why stained glass windows look so elegant. In paintings, the buffer may be greenish gray, reddish gray, bluish gray—not necessarily just gray.

When painting masses of flowers and foliage, plan the hard and soft edges carefully to create effects of delicacy and crispness. Use many big blurs. Do not paint each individual flower. Pick a few to render accurately in order to define the character of various species, such as roses or lilies, and merely suggest the rest. Thus will you escape being tedious.

Paint on gray days. Colors are much more intense when there is no direct sunlight—there are no harsh contrasts of light and shade. With flower markets the important thing is color, not lights and darks.

Make good use of hard, taut, geometric man-made objects such as pavements, awnings, umbrellas, poles, to offer contrast and to emphasize the random delicacy of the flowers.

Of the flower markets shown here, two are in Valencia, one is in Paris, and all three portray rainy Sunday mornings with lots of wet pavement, lovely reflections and gray eerie light.

The figure shopping for plants in the Ile de la Cité picture is my wife, Mary. Her interest in gardening in real life is limited to watering the African violets on the kitchen windowsill. Although she poses for me often in the photographs I take for research, she is usually a stand-in to give me the scale for a burro or an old crone to be inserted in the setting. Mary rarely appears as herself in a painting. Even here, she is a stand-in for a real gardening aficionado.

Plate 7. ILE DE LA CITÉ—Paris

Plate 8. OLD LADY IN BLACK —Valencia

I had arrived in the town of Albaída, Spain, early one winter morning and had been combing its streets for a promising painting location. I was tired and ready to regard the day's accomplishment as having eliminated Albaída as a source for picture material when I came upon this scene. I knew immediately that the composition was a natural. I examined it with delight.

The road sloped up to the left, furnishing a platform for the main figures as well as a diagonal line to complement the parallel one formed by the tree. That wonderful shaggy tree provided

Plate 9. CONVERSATION

strong textural contrast to the solid buildings. The buildings retreated in a zigzag pattern to produce interesting perspective.

Even the light and shade were ideally arranged. The dark lacy shadow on the side wall made a good background for the white burro, as did the glancing light on the far wall for the dark burro and cart.

But the central figures and the burros and the cart weren't at the original scene. Only the boy sweeping up remodeling debris was there. I had seen the foreground figures a block or so away and was able, with a little wine money, to persuade them to continue their conversation in my composition. The burro and cart had to be transplanted from a distant village by the magic of paint.

Mary and I were traveling in Spain between Valencia and Alicante searching for subject matter. There was a leaden sky and the countryside looked monochromatic and uninspiring. On gray days, romantic, picturesque Spain, with its brilliant white stucco walls, shimmering olive leaves, ultramarine skies and ochre hills, becomes poor, suffering, primitive Spain with gray walls, gray trees, gray skies and gray hills.

We turned off the main road to take a shortcut to the small city of Alcoy where we planned to spend the night. Suddenly, across a deep ravine, we came upon this scene of Onteniente. We saw a string of ancient rustic cubes scattered along the edge of a cliff—buildings that had grown there like crystals hundreds of years ago. Even in flat dim light there was a sense of texture.

I stopped the car and studied what I saw. I walked about imagining how this village would appear in glancing sunlight. I consulted the compass and calculated the time of day when the sun would be in the correct position to produce such an effect. Then we proceeded to nearby Alcoy to wait for the morning sunlight.

Next day—more gray skies. A chance to explore inner resources, Agatha Christie, gin rummy, incomprehensible Spanish TV and good sherry.

Next day—still more gray skies. More reading and card playing. No museums, no castles, just flat agricultural landscape.

Next day—again, gray skies. Onteniente had better be good!

Next day—brilliant sunlight. Romantic Spain was back.

We moved on to Onteniente immediately in case the compass calculations were wrong. They weren't. The scene exceeded expectations. Not only were the rays of the sun picking up the structure and texture of the buildings, but they were making three-dimensional shapes of the bushes cascading down the ravine. And, as if that weren't enough, a goatherd with his flock was descending a path to the bottom in exactly the right compositional location.

This scene yearned to be painted. I took many photographs while the effect lasted and tried to burn the image into my memory.

During the remainder of the trip we searched conscientiously for other inspiring locations but the urge to return home and begin painting Onteniente kept intruding. Weeks later, the painting reproduced here was finally executed. But there were changes made along the way. The deep blue sky, so welcome after such a siege of gray, had destroyed the original El Greco "Toledo in a Storm" effect, so it was replaced by dramatic clouds seen and painted from my studio window.

And the little goatherd and his goats failed to provide enough interest to overcome the boredom of a cliffside of scrub pine bushes—third dimension or no—so the final painting was cropped and only the top half saved.

Plate 12. GRANADA PRODUCE STALL

The central figure in this painting of a Granada produce stall is the little boy. Except for the burro, he is the only passive figure in the picture. The stallkeeper is reading, the ladies are shopping, the two men are rushing down on errands, the girl is retrieving something. The little boy is still—but not for long.

There are two reasons why I like scenes where the streets consist of steps. One is that the buildings are placed on different levels at erratic angles, producing a variety of irregular light patterns and complicated perspectives. The other is that I am likely to find donkeys. Motorized vehicles can't make it up and down those steps.

Plate 10. ONTENIENTE

Here is a broad view looking down on the little produce stand shown on the previous page. It illustrates even better the possibilities for composition that a hodgepodge of planes and angles can afford.

This plaza is still one of my favorite painting locations, even though on my latest visit I saw that the demolition crews had been at work. The photograph shows that the center buildings had been pulled down, and the rubble was still there.

Plate 13. GRANADA PLAZA

Plate 14. MULES OF TARANCÓN, STANDING

    The village is Tarancón, between Valencia and Madrid. The time is mid-morning on a gray day. There is no sunshine, no shadow, but there is soft subtle color to see—golden ochres and rusts.
    The man has disappeared into a house, leaving the mules to wait. The neighbor ladies are enjoying a leisurely chat. The man comes out—he is slipping behind schedule. He hurries away down the hill, wheels rattling.

Plate 15. MULES OF TARANCÓN, RUNNING

This scene has a quiet, lonely mood broken only by the sound of the gentle surf and the muffled shouts of the fishermen returning with their catch. They ply their trade as did their ancestors when a watchtower standing on the high cliff in the distance once warned of hostile invaders from the sea. Now they will go up to the village to hawk their fish to the housewives and this afternoon they will be back scraping their boats and mending their nets. By then the tourists will have descended and the fishermen will be sharing this loveliest of beaches with hundreds of oily bodies lying on towels or running around kicking sand into the eyes of those lying on towels.

The painting was made with the help of memories and snapshots taken when I was visiting Torremolinos in 1958—long before it became densely packed with high-rise hotels and condominiums. I came to know the fishermen by chance. One morning I was nearby when an unexpected rough wave tipped a boat and impaled a man's inner thigh on an oarlock. My car and I were pressed into service to take him to Málaga for emergency treatment. I spent the morning drinking brandy and coffee with his friends while waiting to take him home. They are simple proud people living in a dual culture with the wealthy tourists. Nobility of spirit has nothing to do with affluence.

I haven't been back, but I'm told that the hundreds of beach bodies have become thousands. I wonder if at dawn the shore still belongs to the fishermen, or if they have succumbed to this final invasion.

Plate 16. TORREMOLINOS AT DAWN

Plate 17. CASA SUECIA (Swedish House)

There is a sunny Spain full of color—bullfights, flamenco dances, and everywhere fiestas. It is the Spain of the travel posters. But there is another Spain in the south which is dusty and poor and melancholy. It is Moorish Spain with its black dresses, white buildings, ochre earth and plaintive music.

But beauty can be found even in a garbage cart and an old crone picking at her ultimate tooth. Think of this scene as an arrangement in black and tan. Colorful Spain is represented by the blue "Casa Suecia" sign and the red pom-pom.

Plate 18. ALTEA (detail–girl)

This painting gave me a chance to play with textures and paint effects. The scene's back lighting produced sparkling reflections on the pebbled walkways, smooth walls and tile roofs. To achieve this effect of strong light, thick heavy paint was troweled on with a palette knife in the sunlit areas to put them in relief, so that they might catch more than their share of the light shining on the finished picture. Thick paint also has the advantage of adding a feeling of third dimension to a painting.

The old walls were in flat shadow. Here it was important to use thin paint, even though the actual texture was impasto, in order to avoid the bumps that would catch unwanted light. The water-washed streaks were made by pressing a big brush laden with a little paint and a lot of turpentine against the canvas at the top, so that the liquid trickled down as rain would have done on the wall itself.

When it comes to painting methods, I am not a purist. There are those who confine themselves to paint brushes and knives to be used in the traditional manner. I am not averse to using anything that will produce the effect I want, be it splatter screens, Kleenex or even gravity. Did you ever, in the first grade, pass a toothbrush with paint on it over a piece of window screen to splatter dots onto a stencil? I still do.

Altea is a lovely fishing village on the Spanish Costa Blanca. It cascades in tiers down the side of a steep hill. The difficulty in building large hotels on such terrain had thus far spared Altea the fate of her beach-level neighbors.

Plate 20. ALTEA (detail—wall)

Plate 19. ALTEA

Plate 21. THE GIRL AND THE CAT

The child has been given some kind of food which she's playing with. She has it in her lap. We don't know what it is, but the cat knows and is waiting.

Here's a subtle example of Ivanowski's law about tension versus relaxation. Both figures are motionless, but while the child is sitting quietly munching her snack, the cat is poised with tense anticipation to spring for a discarded scrap.

One time at a large art show I exhibited a little painting of a baby burro tied to a pole. It was sandwiched between two major paintings of Western wild animals. I was approached by a lady telling me how disappointed she was not to have seen it before it was sold because she empathized so with the little fellow. Then she said, "But I love cats, too. If you ever do a painting of some cats, please keep me in mind."

Two or three years later, I came upon this windowful of frisky kittens with their mother in an abandoned hut and decided to paint them. When the picture was finished, I sent a photo of it to the lady for her consideration. She returned it with a short note: "I meant lions or cougars!"

Plate 22. FAMILY PORTRAIT

The setting for this painting is on the Greek island of Rhodes. Since we spent part of our honeymoon there, we decided to keep the picture to recall happy memories and it hangs in our living room.

When we decide to keep a picture for ourselves, we don't make an effort to give it an official name. It becomes *That Greek Tree Picture* or *That Old Car Picture*. Sometimes it is sent on loan to a show and temporarily acquires a respectable name like *Olive Tree of Rhodes* or *Restaurante Vicente*, but when it returns it once again becomes *That Greek Tree Picture* and *That Old Car Picture*.

People like to ascribe colors to the light in different places. In the south of France it is pink, in New Mexico it is blue and in Greece it is white. My scant scientific background tells me that the color of the light varies with the size of the particles in the air and the different wave lengths that are refracted through them. It also tells me that the human brain is susceptible to suggestion, so that the pink earth and pink granite buildings make the light in Provence seem pink, the whitewashed buildings and whitewashed walls and whitewashed sidewalks make the light in Greece seem white, and the dark blue sky in New Mexico makes the light seem blue. Whatever the reasons, I see the unconscious evidence in my own paintings.

Plate 23. THAT GREEK TREE PICTURE

Plate 24. GREEK WOMEN WASHING

It was late November, early in the morning and frigid. I came upon these women washing clothes in a wide shallow stream that must have been like liquid ice. Perhaps it was the mist in the air that made me see and paint a blue-white light, perhaps it was the time of day, or perhaps it was simply my desire to express COLD!

Plate 25. WHITE ROSES WITH ONION

Still life painting is very satisfying because the artist is able to control all the elements. He can select whatever he wants to paint according to his mood and to what is at hand—an exquisite vase, an intricately carved bowl, an old pot. He can gather together all his favorite objects collected over the years: dolls, carvings, fabrics, glassware; combine them with fruits, flowers, fish, anything; and at his leisure select, arrange and light them to his satisfaction.

Then he paints his picture under studio conditions, where the wind doesn't blow, the light doesn't change, and there are no curious passersby. Complete concentration is possible. The objects don't move or get tired or bored, and there is no need to cope with the rigidity and distortion encountered when working from photographs. Once in a while a rose may wilt or a grape may rot or a fish may get a bit ripe, but they can be replaced.

The artist has time to play around with various techniques used by masters ranging from Harnett to Cezanne to Braque. Or he can take his inspiration from the exciting bravura style of Fechin or the personal, delicate manner of Pushman.

It is impossible to place a rose in a setting where its beauty doesn't radiate. These two paintings show white roses in different lights. One painting has flat lighting which delineates the subtle values of the petals, and the other painting has strong back lighting which plays up the fragile transparency of the petals and the firm structure of the flowers themselves. In both these paintings, I set the aristocratic roses in crude pottery vases. In one painting, an onion nestles beside a fine Chinese porcelain box.

Plate 27. CHRYSANTHEMUMS

Plate 26. BACKLIT ROSE

Plate 28. THE SPIRIT LAMP

Once I thought that the elements of a still life should be related or at least logical companions—elegant things together, rustic things together, never mixed. I no longer think this. It is enough that they harmonize visually to produce beauty and interest. Their relative social status is beside the point. As I look at these last three still lifes, which were painted several years apart, I notice that they all contain the same color combinations: purple, yellow, green and white. And they all contain similar objects: grapes, silver, onions and crystal. Please strike any claim that I never repeat myself!

I love the character of the little spirit lamp. It was a special wedding present and I will someday paint it lighted. In the final still life, I seem to have expanded my usual color scheme to include peach.

Plate 29. STILL LIFE WITH VIOLETS

As I have mentioned, my first teacher, Ivanowski, was a portrait painter, so it was natural that I should pursue such a career. For a while I did so and it was a good time for me. I painted largely in Louisiana, where the ante-bellum period had established a tradition of having family portraits made and where portrait painters were respected guests. I made and have kept many fine friends from my years there. But there is great pressure in painting portraits. It is not enough that the picture be well-painted. It is not enough that it be a fine likeness. It must also be, protestations to the contrary, a flattering likeness and one that conforms to the way sitters and their families think they look. If the result is not successful, after many tries, the painter goes unpaid and is unhappy. There is no market for a rejected portrait.

An easel painting is one that is produced for its own intrinsic value and is not contracted for in advance. Portraits of one's friends and loved ones are easel paintings because there is no contract and no guarantee is given. Failures are discarded. "Let's try another time, thanks for posing." No pressure. But although this painting of Mary and Elizabeth and our dog, Pauline, was done under the relaxed atmosphere of an easel painting, there were, nevertheless, very difficult physical conditions. We were living in a tiny apartment in Santa Fe where I had a ten-by-eleven-foot studio. While working on this almost four-foot square portrait, I frequently had to haul it out to the living room to study it from a good viewing distance.

The unconscious desire to flatter is a special handicap for an artist striving to paint good likenesses of members of his family. Mary's face was giving me great trouble. I kept checking and rechecking the drawing and could not find the error. Finally, in desperation, I sent an S.O.S. to Bettina Steinke, a fine portrait painter and good friend. She took one look and said, "Put a darker shadow under that nose and make it stick out the way it really does."

Likeness is no longer a problem with this painting. Mary has changed her appearance by cutting her long hair, Elizabeth has grown up, and the dog has died.

Plate 30. MARY, ELIZABETH AND PAULINE

Plate 31. ELIZABETH, BABY

I began doing portraits of Elizabeth when she was a tiny baby. I put her on her stomach at the edge of a bed and painted this "Gerber's Baby Food" picture. For Mary's Christmas when Elizabeth was a year and a half, I painted the next one. At eight, Elizabeth posed for this one with our kitten, Feather, and at twelve, she was my subject for this smiling picture which hangs in our kitchen. Shown on the next page, is the most recent portrait, painted when Elizabeth was sixteen.

Plate 32. ELIZABETH, 1½ YEARS

Plate 34. ELIZABETH, 12 YEARS

Plate 33. ELIZABETH AND FEATHER, 8 YEARS

When I was eighteen years old and studying with Ivanowski, I had graduated from painting plaster casts and cyclamens to painting live models. Finally came the time when he thought I might be ready to try a real portrait under his supervision, and we drafted my mother into service as a sitter. He knew that she was from Spain and asked if she had something Spanish to wear; she selected her shawl. It is one of the regrets of my life that the portrait has been lost. Ivanowski's "supervision" was more accurately a demonstration lesson. The portrait was painted mostly by him—and it was wonderful.

Very old Spanish shawls of embroidered silk are not really Spanish, they are Chinese. Indeed, the motifs are Chinese figures and pagodas. Along with rice, the shawls were products of the clipper ship trade between Spain and China. This one was given to my mother's grandmother one hundred and fifty years ago.

I had been seeking an idea for a "showpiece" painting to enter in a group exhibition when the thought occurred to me to do a picture using that old shawl. I borrowed the shawl from my mother and put it around the shoulders of our daughter Elizabeth who had just turned a very grown-up sixteen. Her dark eyes, her dark hair, and the elegant shawl made an inspired combination. I posed her with her face in shadow so that the picture would really be a portrait of the shawl. But the likeness is there.

My mother gave the shawl to Elizabeth for her sixteenth birthday.

Plate 35. THE SPANISH SHAWL

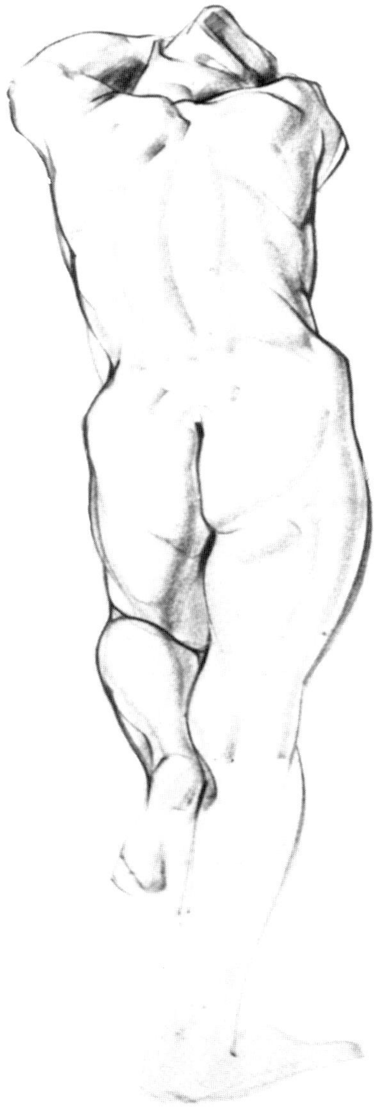

DRAWING

Everything begins with drawing, whether it be the fledgling attempts of an art student or the confident execution of a master painter.

In an art class, the purpose of drawing is to teach the eye to see proportion, form and values of light and dark. The eye transmits an image to the brain and the brain tells the hand to move the pencil to delineate what the eye sees. The hand can't do it the first time, or the second, or at all, until it has had lots of practice. The first day in drawing class the brain says, "Hand, draw that plaster statue." Hopeless result! The brain orders again and keeps ordering but begins supplementing the orders with a little helpful information about proportion and shading and gradually the hand improves. Then the brain says, "Draw that live model." Then, "Draw some more models." Then, "Draw some models with clothes on, draw those landscapes, those boats, draw the detail on that cathedral, draw those Yugoslavian peasants, draw that old man...."

One day the brain says, "Let's drop the pencil and the pen and see if you can do it with a brush—we'll call it wash drawing. Take a cake of black watercolor paint and a little water. Draw the models, draw that church, draw that Arab's back...."

Then the brain begins thinking about and experimenting with color. The hand need only obey simple instructions: "More yellow, sky grayer...." The painter has now taken the step from wash drawing to watercolor painting.

Segovia

Drawing is a good starting point because a beginner using a pencil can make a statement without being encumbered by messy and difficult painting materials. But even after one has become adept at handling paint, drawing remains a starting point. Here are two examples. A watercolor painting of Montana Clydesdales distributing hay was planned out with pencil drawings, of which this is one. The oil picture of an Egyptian donkey pulling logs (Plate 147) was painted over the careful drawing shown here. But the lines are not merely "filled in" with paint. The drawing skills have been transferred to paint so that the brush, now laden with oil color, continues to draw.

Drawing can be a learning medium, it can be a preliminary step to a painting, or it can, with beauty of line and texture, be an end in itself.

After painting portraits for a while, I went to New York to satisfy a need I felt for further study. There I soon realized the limitations of portrait painting. I was young and thrilled by the great big world of art I saw around me. Illustration, especially, fascinated me; telling stories was more fun than painting likenesses. So after art school I turned to illustration and spent several years painting covers for paperback books and record albums. I made a fine living but eventually became tired of working at the direction of others. I often thought about the paintings that I grew up with. I was still making regular visits to my favorites at the Metroplitan Museum. And I used to think about the year I spent in Santa Fe, New Mexico, watching the artists there paint figure studies, street scenes, still lifes, anything they wanted. They had little money but they were free.

A short trial stay in Europe painting landscapes persuaded me to make a break. I knew two things: that I was taking a chance by giving up my established career because the market for easel paintings was very weak, and that I had to become a much better outdoor painter before I could hope for success. Easel painting calls for a different mental approach and for different skills than do portrait painting and illustration. I was ill-equipped. But strong desire canceled thoughts of risk and I set off for a year's study abroad.

The year stretched out to almost three. I roamed from northern Norway to southern Egypt and all points between, wherever there was a good picture gallery or picturesque scenery. I rented a studio in Florence for ten months and hired my own models. I studied composition and painting techniques in Dusseldorf for six more months. I painted in watercolor because oil paintings take forever to dry and often require working outside in the cold. Watercolors can be painted from the front seat of a car with the heater on and they dry for instant packing.

One of the mysteries of the art business is that watercolor painting is so underrated in comparison to oil. It is a permanent medium, rag paper being very durable, and it keeps its crispness and freshness indefinitely—just like a raspberry stain on a white linen suit. The difficulties in producing a really good watercolor can hardly be imagined by an oil painter.

The oil painter can work any way he wishes. He can first cover the canvas with a neutral wash and then block in the darkest darks, the lightest lights and the strongest colors. With these anchors established, he can gauge intermediate values and color correctly. He can paint the same brush strokes over and over until they look both accidental *and* accurate. His paint will stay wet for hours, even days.

The watercolorist has no such luxury. If he is to keep his painting spontaneous and sparkling, he must work from light to dark, always careful not to touch areas of the paper which are to remain white. He must be sure of his values in advance because he will have only one chance to get them right. He must work quickly and deftly because the paint dries almost instantly.

We know from the watercolors of Turner, Sargent and Flint that the medium can be used to create masterpieces which can stand with pride alongside any oil. And, because of the extraordinary discipline required, it is also excellent training for oil painting. It requires the joint skills of drawing with the brush and planning out a whole picture in advance.

What competence I possess as an oil painter I feel I owe to the years I spent working exclusively in watercolor. My ultimate choice of a medium is oil because I am still under the spell cast by my first teacher, Ivanowski, and by my collection of painter-idols. Had I fallen originally under the influence of Sir Russell Flint, I have no doubt that I would be primarily a watercolorist. The reason I paint very few watercolors today is that I find the transition in thinking to be a great strain. I must work many days at the watercolor board, changing my mental fix, before I begin to produce anything that I might consider saving.

In order to capture the feeling of the entrance to this beautiful old Mexican mission, the values and colors had to be worked out carefully in advance to give an effect of light and shade with the sun just glancing across the surface of the building. I worked all this out in small test sketches.

Pools of the selected paints were mixed up in jars and washed on with a wide brush. White areas were saved with the aid of liquid mastic applied ahead of time and peeled off after the washes were dry. The figures around the door and over the window, the railings, the intricate carving on the facade, all required careful rendering in paint over accurate pencil drawing. Everything cannot be done with broad, spontaneous washes. But with thoughtful advance planning the painting can avoid a labored look.

The old lady in black was introduced to furnish scale and interest.

Plate 36. SAN JOSÉ MISSION—San Antonio

Plate 37. WATERCOLOR ROSES

I once spent a few months studying in an art school in Dusseldorf, Germany, with a man named Hans Georg Lenzen. His special talent was to teach the students how to stimulate their imaginations, how to take ideas from their surroundings and, in short, how to see.

He would ask us to bring to class a variety of objects whose shapes and patterns attracted us, such as a pine cone, a fish, an unusual rock, or a squash. Then he would show us how to study them. We would change their scale or color, or would choose arbitrarily to represent one as solid mass and overlap it with another drawn with a feathery line.

Another exercise he fancied was to have us paint with watercolors on glass, press paper onto the glass, and refine the resulting abstract blotches into recognizable shapes, much the way children lying on their backs on a hillside find images in moving clouds. His aim was to teach us to see shapes, to redesign nature rather than copy it, and to recognize and make use of happy accidents when they occur.

One day he directed me to scumble an interesting broken surface onto a piece of watercolor paper. The next morning he walked into the room with a couple of roses, which he put in a drinking glass in front of me. He said, "Load up a brush with paint, place it on its side against the paper and rotate it to convey these flowers in the Japanese fashion." After a morning's practice, before the roses wilted, I came up with this painting. It now hangs in our home.

This happy accident was made to happen, with the help of Hans Georg Lenzen.

Plate 38. CHURCH AT TRAMPAS—New Mexico

This picture was shown at The National Academy of Western Art annual exhibition. Mary had wanted to keep it because one of those little children in the background is our daughter, Elizabeth, but the painting had to be given up because I was committed to send a piece and it was all I had. Somewhat against our hopes, it was sold out of the show.

Later we became friends with the buyers but didn't realize they owned the painting until we saw it in their home. When Mary said, "You have a painting we wished we could have kept," they immediately offered to trade it for something else they liked as much. So again we own the picture with our little girl in it, small though the figure is.

When I went to Trampas to do this painting there were no goats around, as there had been on a previous visit, so some goats from an old photo I had taken in Spain had to substitute.

Plate 39. INDIAN MARKET

Every August in Santa Fe there is an Indian Market weekend. Indians from all over the Southwest bring their beautiful handcrafted wares such as Kachina dolls, pots, paintings, weavings and jewelry. They enter them in competitions the night before the market opens and then, long before dawn, the center of town is given over to booths and stalls and the hustle of sales preparation.

Some, like the women of this picture, with only limited works to sell, can manage with a folding table and chair or even a couple of blankets. But for the lady in the foreground, something extra is needed. The quality and value of her merchandise require a portable safe.

I remember this man well because he denounced me to the police of his remote Yugoslavian village. Although he had acquiesced with a nod to my "May I take your picture?" sign language, he later claimed that I was molesting and mocking him with my camera. After I spent three hairy hours in a detention cell awaiting an interpreter, the matter was cleared up. My German license plates were to blame. The Yugoslavian iron curtain had just been lifted to Western tourists and the memories of wartime brutality were still fresh.

Plate 40. MAN OF PLAV

Plate 41. EGYPTIANS

Plate 42. KONYA MOSQUE

Plate 43. CHURCH—Rieka, Yugoslavia

Plate 44. PARIS VIGNETTE

Plate 45. YUGOSLAVIAN STREET PHOTOGRAPHER

Yugoslavia was my introduction to the Moslem world. It was the first country I had ever visited with a culture different from our own. I was on my way to explore the countries of the Middle East, planning to drive through one after another around the eastern Mediterranean. I would see Turkey, Syria, Lebanon, Israel and Egypt.

As a teenager, I had discovered the work of Dean Cornwell and his mentor, Frank Brangwyn. I especially loved their paintings of Egypt and the Holy Land. I had always wanted to visit that part of the world. My money was running low and it looked as if this might be the last time for a while that such a trip would be possible for me.

The year was 1959. The United States was out of favor with the Arab states for having sided against them in a crisis over the Suez Canal. Egypt and Syria had joined forces and tension between them and Israel was, as usual, at a breaking point. It was hardly a propitious time for one person in an old Opel car to be roaming around those countries.

There was a need for visas and I was told that Vienna was the most likely place to obtain them. In planning my trip, I found that the shortest route from Vienna to Turkey was through Hungary, Romania, and Bulgaria, still closed to Western tourists. The most direct route open was straight down the center of Yugoslavia, along the empty plain—direct but not interesting. So I chose to travel down the Dalmation Coast, visiting the ancient cities of Rieka, Split and Mostar on my way to Dubrovnik.

This was a good decision because those cities, engaged in maritime trade, have always been somewhat European in culture. The weaning away from my own food and language was gradual.

In our day when sophisticated copy equipment and photographic processes are commonplace, it is interesting to come upon an old street photographer who earns his living with an ancient view camera. He makes copies of daguerreotype portraits and documents for people, using the sun as his source of light. This painting is of such a man standing in front of a shabby wall. The remnants of placards and posters clinging to the wall make a lovely textured background.

I saw this tiny chapel as I was driving south into Dubrovnik. The month was December and it was rainy and cold. The days were short, it was getting dark, and I was tired. I was anxious to get into town to the haven of a hotel and the comfort of a hot bath when I saw this small church reflected in the wet pavement.

The bath would have to wait. I painted sitting in the front seat of my car with the windshield wipers going. As I was finishing, the figure in the yellow slicker passed by, so I squeezed out some opaque white, mixed in a little yellow, ignored the purist principles of transparent watercolor, and dashed him in.

Dubrovnik turned out to be a delightful city of medieval origins. Only foot traffic is permitted within its walls. It reminded me of an Italian city, not surprising considering its long history of commerce with Venice and Bari. I spent several days there painting watercolors and basking in the sun.

Plate 46. LITTLE CHAPEL AT DUBROVNIK

Plate 47. DUBROVNIK CATHEDRAL

This particular watercolor was painted in the town square from a small alcove hidden off to one side. As I was working, I was interrupted by a beautiful statuesque elderly woman dressed in well-cared-for, pre-war clothes of classic design. With Victorian elegance and a slight arrogance, she addressed me in two or three languages before settling on English. She asked if I painted miniature portraits on ivory. She had a photograph which she wanted copied in oils onto a piece of ivory which could be placed in a locket. I said that I was sorry but I had no experience painting on ivory.

She replied, "I am sorry, too. I've looked so long for someone to paint my miniature for me." And with that, she made a gesture of frustration toward this watercolor and added, "Anybody can do that!"

Plate 48. MARKET SCENE I—Skopje

Plate 49. MARKET SCENE II—Skopje

Several years after my visit, Skopje was destroyed completely by a massive earthquake, so this market does not now exist as I knew it. When I was there, the central section was one long street lined with booths and populated by the kinds of people you see in these two watercolors—people sitting on the ground selling farm produce, gourds, pumpkins and the like.

Later, at home, I looked at the dozens of photographs and sketches I had made and decided that these patterned vignette pictures would be a much more interesting representation of the market than would a solid picture with a lot of people jumbled together on a flat plane.

On the outskirts of the Skopje market there were meeting places where animals and empty carts were left, ready for the trip home after the goods had been sold and the purchases had been made. This one, with the mosque in the background seen faintly through the heavy smoke, made an exotic scene worth painting.

Plate 50. OUTSKIRTS OF THE SKOPJE MARKET

Plate 51. COVERED POOL—Istanbul

Besides the Arab alphabet, which made ordering a meal somewhat of a lottery, there were other differences in culture to which I had to adjust as I crossed the mountains of Yugoslavia into the Moslem world. By the time I arrived in Turkey, I was used to the clothing: the skull caps, the baggy trousers, and the veils. I was used to the architecture, particularly that of the churches with their beautiful tile domes and their spidery minarets. I was used to hearing the language and had even begun learning a few necessary words such as "men's room" and "how much" and "too much" and, of course, the numbers. But I never quite got used to the plaintive music or to the mournful calls to worship regularly broadcast from the minarets.

The men would respond to those calls, leaving their shoes outside the mosques before entering. Everywhere there were covered pools like this one where they could wash their feet in order not to risk offending Allah. There is grace and charm even in a building of such lowly function.

Istanbul is a city that should be explored on foot. On my first visit, I had an opportunity to do so and to paint many pictures, especially of the back streets and of vendors near the harbor. Mary was with me on my second visit. Our cruise ship made a one-day stop there. We took a taxi tour of the mosques and spent a couple of hours in the bazaar. My aplomb as a second-time visitor was shattered in that teeming labyrinth when all the lights went out, and stayed out.

I remember this particular morning in Konya. It was bitterly cold but there was a beautiful dusty yellow light piercing the smoke from the wood-burners. It silhouetted the black carriage with the white horses, the bicycle rider and the street pole. There were carriages all over the city. Most were taxis.

Here is another case where other people's backwardness and misery profited me greatly. As I listened to the clip-clop of horses' hooves and to the hacking coughs of the inhabitants, I thought how modern vehicles and clean air laws would improve their lives but rob this scene of its picturesqueness.

Plate 52. CARRIAGE TAXI—Konya, Turkey

Plate 53. QUARRY CART—Mersin, Turkey

This painting, done in Mersin, was put up for resale at an auction of Western Art in New York City and was chosen by the directors of an Arizona bank for their collection of Western art. I hope this revelation of the scene's true location will not diminish the painting in their eyes.

The southern coast of Turkey, when I visited it, had not been excavated; Roman things were often dug up by farmers with their plows. Little farm boys would flag down the occasional car along the highway to hawk authentic Roman coins. I bought a few coins but my major purchase was a beautiful Roman bowl I found in a tiny village antique shop. When I stopped in Antioch that night, I found that the hotel mantelpiece was decorated with eight bowls identical to mine, except that they had not yet been artificially aged. My first reaction was to feel cheated. However, I soon came to appreciate the hours of workmanship spent to age the bowl and knew I had made a good purchase. It is beautiful and has graced our home for many years.

From Antioch, I drove east inland to Aleppo, Syria. But my grand ambition to record the Middle East with sketch pad and camera was not to be realized. Back in Ankara I had picked up some kind of infection which had been slowly draining my energy and resolve. It could no longer be ignored. So I made a beeline for Beirut where I had friends who could find me good medical care.

My hope of seeing the Holy Land was also dashed when I discovered that an Israeli stamp in a passport prevented entry into Egypt. Since a stay in Egypt did not preclude a future visit to Israel, I chose to go to Egypt.

Once well, I put my car on a boat for Alexandria, drove to Cairo, and after a few days boarded an overnight train for the three hundred mile trip to Luxor.

It looked as though I wouldn't be able to spend even one night in Luxor. I had inadvertently arrived when the Coptic Christmas was being celebrated and, since Luxor is the center of the Coptic Christian community, people from all over the Middle East had traveled there to celebrate the holiday. There wasn't a hotel room to be had, so I booked a berth on the northbound train back to Cairo.

I spent the day rushing around—saw the temples of Karnak and Luxor, crossed the river to the Valley of the Kings to see the Palace of Nefertiti, King Tut's tomb, and more temples—until finally it was time to collapse onto the train.

But at the last minute, someone told me about an Arab rest house across the river where I might find a bed for the night. The bed I found was clean but there was no water, no electricity, no English, and strange food. Luckily, a couple of Arabic-speaking French road engineers were billeted there and they helped me make arrangements to stay. I stayed six weeks!

I wandered about taking photographs and painting watercolors. There were crews working with camels, harvesting sugar cane. There were cotton fields irrigated with water from ancient wells pumped by oxen urged on with whip flicks by small boys. Their wailing, timeless chants were answered by young colleagues half a mile away.

One day I painted this watercolor of the Temple of Karnak with the horse-drawn carriage taxis that shuttled tourists to and from the hotel.

Plate 54. TEMPLE OF KARNAK—Luxor

Plate 55. LUXOR FERRYBOAT

◀ This is a painting of a ferry with the skyline of Luxor in the background. The large structure is the Temple of Luxor. I am told there is a new hotel on the riverside and I can only hope that it harmonizes with its ancient neighbors.

The painting was exhibited in my one-man show at the Grand Central Art Galleries in New York in October 1965, but it did not sell immediately. Time went by and it languished on the wall. Mary and I were married the following May and one day she happened to say that she loved the painting and hoped it would never sell. I immediately reclaimed it and gave it to her. Soon afterward the gallery called to say that they had just "sold" the painting to someone who had seen it in the show and would I please bring it back. Its new owner, Mary, replied, "Sorry, not for sale!"

The single most important thing impressed on me by all my teachers was that a picture must first be *interesting*. To achieve this, it is necessary to discover good subject matter and to exploit the natural designs and shapes to be found therein. Examples of this might be the adobe cubes in a New Mexico village, the patchwork-quilt meadows of a Connecticut hillside, or the cliffs and boulders of the Grand Canyon. For a painter, there is a special excitement about strange places because there are new shapes to observe and make use of.

Never was there a more fruitful area in this regard than the Middle East. Baggy pants, shawls, robes, fluted domes, minarets, keyhole-shaped openings, and camels are just a few of the eye-catching features to choose from.

So it was with some regret that I put my car back on a boat at Alexandria to cross over to Sicily, passing through the boundary into the Western world—but not before snapping some surreptitious photos of this little Cairo rug merchant reading from a page of the Koran.

Plate 56. CAIRO RUG MERCHANT

Plate 57. THE LONELY MAN

It had been a cold, misty, miserable winter afternoon but the setting sun was finally poking its rays out from beneath the clouds. I had driven around a bend on the coast road when I came upon this workman, soaking wet and still miles from home.

It is a moody, dark picture which for best effect requires a very strong light over it with no glare and preferably no other strong light in the room. Three buyers, one after the other, took the picture home, put it in a glary spot, wondered why they had bought it, and returned it to the gallery. Finally, buyer number four came along and placed it in a dark paneled library with a strong picture light over it.

I did give the lonely man a lift.

I painted the sketch for this rainy scene from a man's living room. I had been working out on the street when it suddenly started raining hard. I began scrambling, trying to fold up my equipment to find shelter. An old gentleman who had been watching me from his window came out and waved me inside. He said, "Why don't you continue your work from my balcony?" He opened some double doors and I sat looking out, nice and dry.

The shower stopped and a man in a proper black funeral suit walked by. He made a very good accent in a rainy day picture full of subtle color. Fortunately, the onslaught of rain had been so sudden that there was no time to take down the laundry.

Plate 58. RAINY STREET—Sicily

Plate 59. RANDAZZO—Sicily

    This is the oldest town still inhabited today that was founded by the Saracens. They conquered Sicily in the 12th century and built this cliffside town. The cliffs were their protection. Those walls shown in the painting were built by them. In seven hundred years they have not fallen down.

The laundry hanging from these city tenements made such a fascinating pattern that I decided to treat my painting as an abstraction which would stand by itself as a good design whether held upside down or sideways. Realism wasn't important. The posters, the balconies, the building blocks, the cobblestones, and the flat gray sky all fit together like pieces of a puzzle.

I chanced to be in Naples many years later and found this same street. Same buildings, same balconies, same cobblestones, same gray sky, different posters, different laundry.

Plate 60. STREET IN NAPLES

Plate 61. SUZY

The nude is the best subject for study. The human body is a magnificently constructed thing. It has a skeleton with tendons and ligaments to hold the bones together. It has muscles that expand and contract to make the parts move and all the parts work in unison. It is covered by a beautiful surface which is the human skin. Best of all, it can be made to stand reasonably still. It is a fantastic teaching medium.

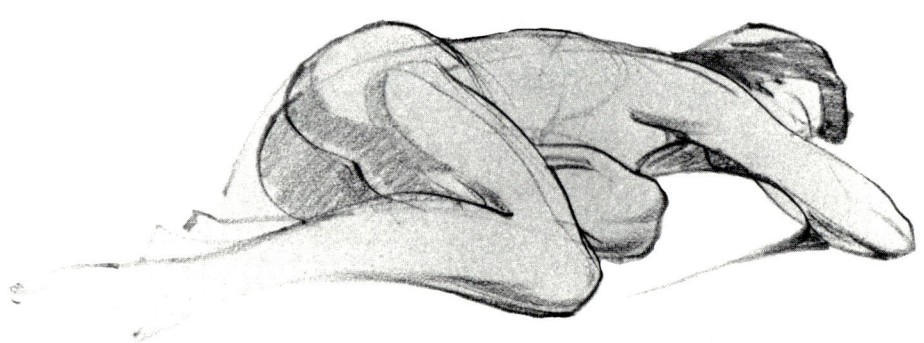

There are linear relationships in the figure to produce rhythm. There are shadow patterns that define the shapes of the individual parts. And there are things to be learned about color from the way light falls on the subtle hues in skin.

But when we artists go out into the world after art school we rarely continue painting what we are best trained to paint—the nude.

◄ What is so rare as a beautiful human body, or so ephemeral? Suzy, who was a model at the Art Students' League when this classroom sketch was made, was once one of "The Three Graces" in the Ziegfeld Follies of 1919.

When I was painting this study, our daughter Elizabeth was ► four years old. She arrived home from playschool one day just as the model was getting dressed and she wanted to know what was going on. When Nancy told her that she had been posing, Elizabeth said she wanted to watch. So it was arranged that we would begin at a later hour the next day. That way we would still be working when Elizabeth got home. She walked in, took one look, and ran to her room to play.

Afterward I asked why she hadn't stayed, and she replied, "She wasn't posing. Posing is standing on your toes." Nothing was said about the model being nude.

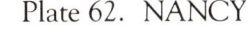

Plate 62. NANCY

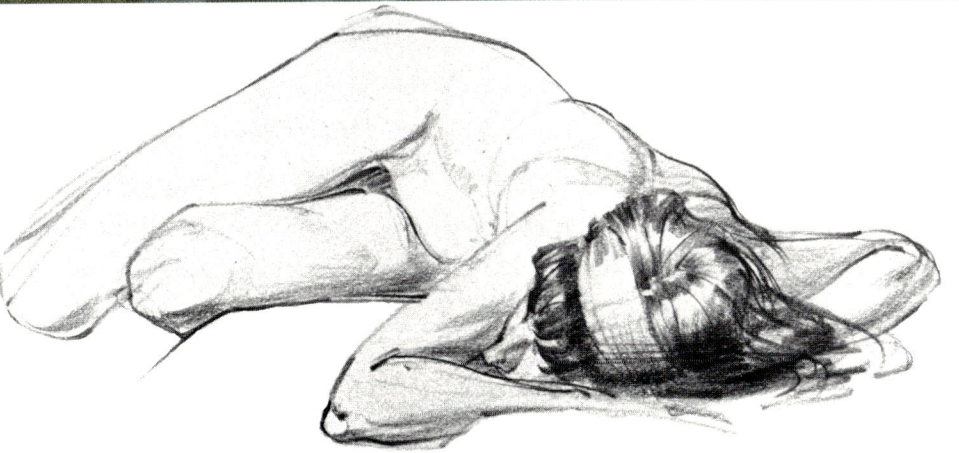

The couple who own this painting will be surprised to see it here with a red background. After this reproduction was made, I decided to paint the background a more subdued color since red can be difficult to live with on a daily basis.

However, Sara was left unchanged. She still seems to be trying to remember whether she turned off the oven.

The man who bought this picture was told by his wife in no uncertain terms that it would have to hang in his office—*inner* office! After a few years, it was home in the master bedroom. But now, I am proud to say, it has finally been elevated to an honored place in a corner of the living room.

Plate 63. SARA

Plate 64. SYLVIA

Plate 65. A ROOFTOP VIEW OF ARGENTAT

Mary has always been a great help to me in my work. She is especially good at tracking down painting locations. While I am painting a field sketch, she reads guidebooks and studies maps. She knows what subjects I like to paint—old buildings, bridges, markets, rustic rural scenes where they still farm with animals—and she knows how to find them. She reads about the agriculture and gets clues to the topography. Grain fields mean flat or gently sloping land with lots of factory farms and tractors. Green areas on the map mean solid forests, not promising for paintings. But small truck farms often mean chopped-up hilly country with plenty of oxen and draft horses; dairy products mean meadows separated by rows of shade trees—good subjects.

Argentat and the countryside around it sounded great in the guidebook: "Situated in a valley of small farms, the town spreads out from both sides of a river spanned by an old stone bridge. Ancient slate-roofed buildings line streets that rise steeply from the water. A church with its tower dominates the town."

We drove considerably out of our way to get there and were richly rewarded. This was my first painting showing both sides of a river. I found it interesting to figure out the shapes and angles and patterns of the roofs and to employ ways to achieve the illusion of third dimension—to create atmospheric perspective.

When I think of France, I see granite buildings. I see tall faded blue double windows lined with lace curtains, and I see pink tile roofs set with lots of chimneys. French architecture is homogenous throughout the country and throughout the ages.

As you drive through regions that were almost totally devastated by war, you discover that the villages still look picturesque. The rebuilding retains the original architectural character because the French have taste and they know how to keep a good thing. Of course, there are some sensational exceptions where the compulsion to be avant-garde seems to prevail over good aesthetic judgment and common sense. The plan to expand the Louvre Museum by building a gigantic glass pyramid in its ancient courtyard comes to mind.

Given a choice, I prefer to paint in areas of the country which escaped destruction, because I like to paint Roman stone bridges and century-old trees and buildings with the patina that only great age can produce.

In the painting shown here, the building displays not only the mellowness of time but also the soft turquoise color left by a copper sulphate spray on some bygone grapevines.

The old lady and the little girl have just finished throwing grain to the chickens.

Plate 66. FEEDING THE CHICKENS

Plate 67. VILLE FRANCHE

This little market is in the town of Ville Franche on the French Riviera near Nice. Between high buildings, the narrow streets rise steeply from the water's edge and are linked to form a kind of giant rabbit warren on the side of a hill.

I climbed upward through the deep, dim alleys, finding lots of tunnels and stairways and other picturesque goodies but no vantage points from which to paint them. Everything was too dark and close. Then, near the top, I came upon this open corner and was rewarded for my climb. The space let the light in and the buildings took on lovely, luminous, grayed-down colors softened by the salt spray. Even the pavement had a mellow sheen.

Here is a panoramic view of another river town called Brantôme. This time the vantage point is low so that the row of houses on the opposite bank is reflected in the slow-moving water.

Mary's research came from a food article singing the praises of the three-star restaurant to be found there. Her interest in cooking and mine in eating provided the bonus of a number of fine painting sites, and I did several field sketches there which became studies for larger paintings. Most French towns that are not tourist resorts are good places for painting because the local people are courteous to artists and respect their privacy, even on a public street. Their attention is usually limited to a furtive glance.

Plate 68. THE RED SWING—Brantôme

One summer we were driving through the Cognac country of France and stopped for our midday meal in the village of Hiersac. The town itself had little to offer in the way of either food or scenery and we were about to push on when my eye was struck by a château in the distance. Out came the paints. Food was forgotten, and I painted this backlit noontime sketch.

Although pleased with my effort, I wondered what the château would look like with side lighting at sunrise. I was to find out two years later on another trip to France when we sought out the Hiersac château and I painted the second sketch.

We were staying in a nearby city and I was at my scene by dawn. I found the period when the sunlight was skimming delicately across the facade of the building to be very short, so the painting required sessions on four successive days. On the final day, I was sitting working when a tiny black speck appeared in the distance from around the back of the château. As it came toward me, I saw that it was an old lady carrying a black umbrella. Always on the lookout for a figure to put in a painting, I photographed her as she approached. When she arrived, she stopped to look at my work. She had hobbled half a mile just to see the painting. Having watched me for four mornings from the window of the château, her curiosity to see what I was doing had finally overcome her.

Then she began to talk. "The château is just a shell," she said. "Only four rooms are used. It was once very prosperous, being the center of vast Cognac vineyards, but many years ago there was a prolonged drought and the land was poisoned. The vines withered and the château was abandoned. Fifteen years ago the present owner bought the place, gambled on the soil and planted new vines which are now flourishing. Perhaps someday the lovely old building will be restored to its former glory. Not likely! Not with today's wicked taxes!"

The chatty little lady then told me about the suffering they had all endured under German occupation during World War II. Her husband had died from five years of forced labor. "We could never understand why they were so cruel to us," she said.

As she left me to go back, I took more photographs. She appears in the painting shown here, which was done later in the studio from my sketch. Perhaps her sad stories explain the dark mood and the melancholy sky.

As I reviewed my paintings of France, the one of Ville Franche turned my mind to markets and street vendors and then to the country where they are still found in great abundance—Mexico. In the United States, markets have been organized into super-efficient chain operations where we push carts down aisles past bins, collecting antiseptic plastic packages for delivery to the trunks of our cars. Poor pickings for the artist.

I've painted markets all over Europe, but in Mexico they are at their most primitive and picturesque. In Mexican villages, flowers and produce are still hauled to town by the growers themselves and sold by them from tables set up in central market locations or from canvas blankets laid out on the ground under the shade of makeshift awnings. They are joined by other one-man enterprises selling such merchandise as fabrics, hardware and basketry. These places of simple commerce, with their strong colors, shapes and patterns, provide wonderful picture material.

Plate 73. THE PINK SERAPE

▲ This composition was solid with good architectural shapes to work with. The light was intense, providing an energetic, staccato effect on the crowds passing in and out of the scene. It was for me to select from what I saw; to choose from the umbrellas, jugs, awnings, people rushing and people idling; to arrange and rearrange them; then to single out one figure as a focal point (the woman wearing the pink serape); and finally to tie everything together and make a picture.

I have visited Mexico often since that first time but, in contrast to other places, I have found only minor changes. There are more cars and vans, fewer animals and more plastic. But it still excites me to paint there. In this *Lower Market* picture, the ▶ densely-packed covered area on the left used to be the open street shown in *The Cloth Vendors*, on a previous page. Gone is my vantage point from which I painted the beautiful church.

When I look at many paintings in this book, I ask myself why I chose a particular site and I realize that the choice was often subliminal. Here the composition was right. The slow, measured pace of the old people in the foreground contrasted with the bustling activity of the market. And San Miguel's magnificent cathedral dominating the town, seemed to preside with serene majesty over the masses of block-shaped buildings scattered at its base. All this struck a responsive chord in me.

Plate 72. CLOTH VENDORS—San Miguel de Allende

Back when I was an illustrator, yearning to become a full-time easel painter, I made a trip to Mexico at the invitation of an artist friend who lived there with his family. I visited Cuernavaca, Taxco, and San Miguel de Allende, where I sketched and took photographs. On my return, I did a series of paintings from that material and took them one by one, as they were finished, to Grand Central Art Galleries, the same gallery I had often visited as a child with my father. I hoped that they would take me on.

The director must have thought I showed promise because his rebuffs were polite and he tried to guide me. "Don't paint mules or burros, don't paint laundry, because most pictures are bought by women, and women don't like burros and don't want laundry hanging in their living rooms." Or, "Don't paint cathedrals. Only Catholics buy pictures of cathedrals so you're automatically limiting your market." And finally, "Don't paint Mexico. We've never been able to sell pictures of Mexico."

The advice didn't take. A few weeks later, I delivered a painting like the one reproduced here. It showed a Mexican cathedral, a Mexican burro and a whole clothesline full of Mexican laundry. While the director was patiently explaining to me once more why I shouldn't be choosing these subjects, a customer of the gallery who had been hovering in the background asked if she could buy the painting. Thus did I begin my first association with a gallery and at the same time learn a valuable lesson—always to paint what interests and inspires me and not to paint just what the prevailing wisdom maintains will sell.

Plate 69.
HIERSAC
CHÂTEAU

Plate 70. HIERSAC CHÂTEAU—(sketch, first visit)

Plate 71. HIERSAC CHÂTEAU—(sketch, second visit)

Plate 74. THE LOWER MARKET

Plate 75. KALEIDOSCOPE

Plate 76. KALEIDOSCOPE (detail—figures)

Each vendor has two large canvas squares, one on which to sit and display wares, and one stretched overhead to provide protection from the sun. These vary in color. Onto this pattern of slanted checkerboards appear the vendors with their piles of fruit and vegetables and a stream of shoppers milling up and down the narrow aisles, judging quality and price, sometimes squatting down to buy. I spent a couple of hours watching the constant change of shapes and colors, likening the scene to a kaleidoscope, the hollow tube containing mirrors and colored glass chips which, when rotated, produces an effect similar to the one before me. So I chose the name *Kaleidoscope* for my unpainted picture.

Once this idea was fixed, planning the picture was great fun. It became a matter of juggling shapes and patches of awnings and sunshine, of adjusting values of bright light, solid shadow and filtered light. Finally, I distributed the "chips" of color—the reds, blues, greens, yellows, pinks, oranges and hues in between—doing all these things to move the viewer's eye and make my "kaleidoscope" rotate.

Plate 77. KALEIDOSCOPE (detail—head)

Plate 78. THE MEXICAN ROSARY MAN

◄ I must confess to an undying gratitude for tarpaulins. To the vendors who use them, they are protection from the glare and heat of the sun. To me, they are excellent ploys to be used in composing pictures. They have wonderful, simple shapes which unify and give interest to vignette paintings like *The Mexican Rosary Man*.

The old Indian is selling religious articles to people visiting the church. The stone pillar is a remnant of the Mixtec temple that once served his ancestors. He uses it as an anchor for his tarpaulin.

What caught my eye was the action of the wind on those tarpaulins. You don't think of wind when you think of Mexico. But here were these people sitting serenely in what would normally be a rather ordinary market scene, while overhead the awnings were being whipped and snapped so that they seemed almost alive. The main actor in this scene was surely the wind.
▼

Plate 79. WINDY MARKET DAY

Plate 80. THE MELON STAND

Besides contributing action to a quiet picture (*The Windy Market Day*) or shape to a vignette picture (*The Mexican Rosary Man*), a tarpaulin can also act simply as a necessary empty space in a very busy picture such as *The Melon Stand*. It can also provide linear perspective to guide your eye back into the distance.

Plate 81. CHAPALA FRUIT VENDOR

Here the trusty tarpaulin performs yet another function. In back lighting, it washes a lovely eerie yellow light over the man and his table of produce. It joins with the tree and the post and the shadows cast upon the ground to form a very paintable light and shade pattern.

That little man in Chapala cutting up the fruit wasn't at all happy to have me there staring at him, taking roll after roll of photos to be sure to catch him in the best gesture. To keep placating him, I bought a good deal more pineapple and watermelon than I needed.

Plate 82. THE GUARDIAN

In places where there are open markets in the middle of town, there is no room for the donkeys, so they are left in what I call "donkey parking lots" somewhere on the outskirts. This lot is high above the city of San Miguel and the picture is called *The Guardian* because the little boy has been charged with guarding these valuable family possessions.

Plate 83. BURRO ALLEY, SANTA FE, 1900

This painting was inspired by a turn-of-the-century postcard I once came across showing Burro Alley, a Santa Fe street that still exists. But how it has changed!

I showed my painting to an old gentleman who remembered the town in those days. He laughed. It seems that this corner was used as a parking place for burros and other draft animals while their masters were busy at market. The little houses at the right and in the distance served the carnal needs of these men after they had sold their goods and tipped a few glasses. The present occupants of the real estate are a respectable movie theater and two luxury hotels.

That dilapidated wooden-wheeled cart on the roof, or one like it, still sits atop the current location of The Old Trading Post, a few doors up the street.

We use the Spanish word "burro" interchangeably with the English word "donkey", so why not the Italian word "asino"? They all refer to the same animal.

My special interest in donkey parking places dates back to my first trip to Sicily. The sketch reproduced here, from a faded slide of the painting, was done from life almost thirty years ago. The little street on the edge of the town of Taormina is no longer used for this purpose. For reasons of cleanliness and traffic efficiency, donkeys are forbidden to enter many villages in countries where they used to abound. I feel sorry for the occasional farmer who has never been able to afford a three-wheeled motorcycle van and still has to use his burro, because now he must park it far off from the marketplace and carry his load piecemeal on his own back.

Plate 84. ASINO ALLEY

Plate 85. SAN MIGUEL WOOD MERCHANT

Here is another fine setting for a painting on the outskirts of a market town. There is a windblown sky and a naked tree forming a lovely pattern. The buildings on the right and the wall on the left provide linear perspective and a frame for the action. The action is a wood merchant and his burros rushing through my setting on their way to sell their loads.

Chichicastenango is a wonderfully strange village. It seems to exist oblivious to the handful of American tourists who appear Wednesday nights to stay at the little hotel and disappear again after visiting the Thursday market. Farmers and craftsmen come in from the outlying settlements, carrying their goods on their backs. Some who come bearing great loads of straw are completely obscured so that they resemble moving haystacks. Women carry baskets of produce on their heads. Not even little children come empty-handed. It is an area so poor that no one can afford a beast of burden.

The religion of the region as practiced today is interesting indeed. The Catholic Church, in order to encourage natives to convert, allowed them to retain some of their pagan rituals and customs and overlooked the continued practice of others. Inside the church on market day, rose petals are strewn about, covering the center aisle. The men you see are swinging cans of burning incense on the steps to the church entrance. From the site of this painting, it's only a short walk to a nearby hill and a stone altar where at one time people and, later, animals and, most recently, chickens were sacrificed.

One of my recollections of the town market was a stall occupied by a coffin-maker. He had a few samples of wooden coffins, simple boxes shaped like those you see in vampire movies, narrow at the foot, sloping outward to accommodate the width of the shoulders. I saw people, usually men, standing to be measured for coffins which they would pick up the following Thursday. They would then carry their coffins home, strapped to their backs, to be stored underneath the house until needed.

Each outlying village in this Indian country has its own local costume. In this picture the men in black wearing the turbans and the women wearing the blue skirts and red shawls are from the same district.

Chichicastenango is the site of a very lovely old rustic hotel whose rooms cascade down the side of a hill. I expect it's almost empty now. At the time of this writing, the country is suffering from considerable political and social upheaval. I am told that this region has been sorely abused.

Plate 86. CHICHICASTENANGO—Guatemala

Plate 87. THE PINK PARASOL

The city of Oaxaca in southern Mexico is ringed with little villages, each one having a different kind of market on a different day of the week. One village is known for its livestock market, another for its pottery, another for its baskets, etc. I have explored all of these villages and, though each one has its own appeal for me, I struck gold when I came upon the little town of Etla. I have already shown two paintings which were set there—*Kaleidoscope* and *The Melon Stand*—and now I show three more.

This corner on the edge of Etla which inspired *The Pink Parasol* fascinated me. There was the old white building on the right, the Reyes Sisters Grocery Store, obviously a social hangout. There was the lovely, spreading cottonwood tree, the dirt plaza with its uneven surface, the road leading off to another village, and there was a mountain in the background. It was two o'clock in the afternoon. The sun was high and the market was over.

I found a place where all the people and animals would have to pass. I made myself inconspicuous and waited for a wonderful inventory of subjects to walk through the scene before my eyes. I was not disappointed. My problem was to choose from an overabundance of good material. But strangely enough, the title figure of the painting, the lady carrying the pink parasol, never went down this road. I found her somewhere else.

Here I would like to digress a bit to the subject of choosing titles. A picture that is going into a major show where you hope it will be remembered requires a distinctive title. It should fix itself in people's minds so that mention of it will conjure up an image of that, and only that, specific picture. For example, had this painting been called *After Market Day* or *Going Home* it might later be confused with another. But the words "pink parasol" describe only this one painting.

Plate 88. THE PLASTIC BAG LADY

The lady was irresistible. I stood out of sight and watched her for a long time. Her feet were tired. She was sitting down on the cool tiles waiting for the bus. She was pleased with her purchases. She carefully pulled them all out onto the sidewalk and repacked them a couple of times.

Market day was over. A late afternoon bus came, and it pretty well cleared out the plaza. The bus driver was packing the roof with the big items—giant baskets, bedsprings, sheets of plywood—and the people were patiently packing themselves inside with their carry-on luggage, much of it cackling, squealing or bleating.

The scene carried me back to a similar trip I'd made years earlier in a third-class bus from Cuernavaca to Taxco. I recommend it only to those who enjoy riding the five o'clock subway from Union Square to 125th Street in New York. But even with all the lurching and meshing of sweaty bodies, with the noises and the smells, there is a dignity.

Having seen the load of happy shoppers off at the bus stop, I was wandering around aimlessly when I saw a lady carrying a basketful of live chickens on her head. I aimed my camera and whom should I see in the viewfinder but a soldier holding a rifle pointed at me. This wasn't an Iron Curtain country or the turbulent Middle East; this was Mexico, our friendly neighbor to the south. I was soon made to realize that my chicken lady has been in front of the police barracks, apparently a photographic no-no. I was hastily escorted with great courtesy but firmness back to my car. No more pictures.

Plate 89. AFTERNOON BUS

Plate 90. VELEZ MÁLAGA COURTYARD

Here the same text might serve the paintings on both these pages. Each one shows a hard-working man leaving on an important or extended trip which warrants the riveted attention of his wife and even the casual attention of the children. Each shows a rude dwelling which is the last occupied section of an abandoned building complex. Each is set in strong light—one in early morning and one at noon.

One scene is in Spain where the patient, willing burro, standing to be heavily loaded, is large and white and typically Andalusian. The other is in Mexico where the patient, willing burro, standing to be heavily loaded, is small and black and typically Mexican.

In each place, someone has fulfilled the need for the beauty of flowers—geraniums on the balcony or tin-can plants around the doorway.

Plate 91. SALTILLO—Mexico

As I was painting this sketch of an abandoned adobe shack near Santa Fe, some dogs began to appear. Dog followed dog as I stood there working. They came out of the "deserted" little house and from around the back. There must have been thirty-five dogs. They weren't vicious dogs. I held my ground and they exhibited curiosity rather than hostility. I continued painting, pausing occasionally to photograph them in different attitudes as they ranged across my scene.

Later, in the studio, I enlarged my sketch to the finished picture shown here with the addition of about a dozen dogs and a black, moody "Wuthering Heights" sky to emphasize the eeriness and loneliness of the broken-down building. Eight or ten days of the time spent on the painting was devoted to those dogs—arranging them, rearranging them, painting them in, painting them out, altering my choices. But when it was finished, the picture didn't please me. There was something wrong.

Luckily, I have a couple of artist friends who are willing to apply their objective, well-trained eyes to an ailing painting and to come up with a diagnosis and a remedy. I called in one of these picture doctors and he spotted the trouble immediately. The sky and the dogs projected contrasting moods. I must choose between Emily Bronte and P.G. Wodehouse. Either the sky or the dogs must go. But my heart was set on both. I couldn't give up the dramatic effect of the black sky, yet I hated to waste all the work and energy I had concentrated on the dogs. Besides, I liked them. So I thought to compromise. I began to remove the dogs one by one, thinking, "Perhaps if I eliminate the dogs that are scratching and leave the ones that are sleeping or just staring, if I take out the ones that are growling at each other and the cute puppies...." In the end I was left with one menacing-looking black Doberman. But even he destroyed the mood by suggesting human habitation, so I sent him off to join his companions. My picture finally fit its title.

Plate 92. TIMELESS ADOBE (sketch)

Plate 93. TIMELESS ADOBE

Plate 94. WOODBEARERS OF CHIMAYO

This is another picture from which an important element was removed, but for different reasons. It was painted during a period of acute gasoline shortage. People everywhere were waiting in long lines by gas pumps. So it was an important occasion in the New Mexico hamlet of Chimayo when an old Phillips Petroleum truck pulled up and parked, in the middle of my view, ready to supply the underground tanks at the little filling station.

Never one to miss a chance for a bit of social commentary, I decided to include the truck. It represented an energy commodity needed to fuel our high-tech, motorized existence—a commodity then being withheld from us by the whims of some far-off Middle Eastern sheiks—and it contrasted dramatically with the string of small burros delivering their loads of an ancient fuel supply, firewood, to the households of the community.

Phillips Petroleum trucks are bright red, a good color for a snow picture, and this was an especially lucky truck for me because it was old and dirty and fit right into my rustic picture. I planned to use the title *Fuel Deliveries*.

But fate stepped in. I had finished the painting in time to send it off to the National Academy of Western Art show, hoping it would win a prize, when the word was passed to me that Mr. Lee Phillips of the petroleum family was to be one of the jurors. The truck had to go. Either my colleagues would chastise me for pandering to the jury, or Mr. Phillips would lobby against my picture because I had represented his company by such a shabby truck. Perhaps both.

If there is anything I like to put into my paintings even more than tarpaulins, it is clotheslines. The opinion of the former director of the Grand Central Art Galleries notwithstanding, women do like paintings of laundry hanging in their living rooms. Everybody likes clotheslines and clothes washing. They symbolize the twin virtues of cleanliness and industry. I like a clothesline because, like a tarpaulin, it makes a very useful compositional foil. This Louisiana cabin would be adrift in a sea of green were it not tied to the edge of the picture by the clothesline. The green would be unrelieved had I not hung up a couple of red and yellow garments. The left side of the house would be blank without something for the sunlight to play on.

A line of clothes is like a light in the window. It says someone is home.

Plate 95. LOUISIANA CABIN

Plate 96. TAXCO HORSEMAN

The lady of this Taxco house has washed those clothes in that tub and hung them up in time to catch the backlighting of the sun, adding some sparkle and brilliance to this otherwise drab scene. The clothesline keeps the horseman from dominating the picture and it frames the little burro.

One early morning I was wandering around the city of Málaga in Spain and came upon this very poor section. In Spanish it is called a barrio. Because there was no plumbing inside the houses, activities involving the use of water were done outside in the street—a woman was industriously washing clothes, a couple of men were shaving, another woman was bathing two little children. I felt like an intruder staring at these exercises, which in my own country are customarily done in private.

My social conscience was pricked by the poverty of the place but I soon became caught up with the intrinsic beauty of the scene. Filtered sunlight gave the sheets silhouetted against the high dark pines an iridescent quality and drew rims of light around the little children going to school. The spots of color from the flowers in tin cans not only had eye appeal but provided a sympathetic note. People with scant means had surrounded themselves with what little beauty they could muster. Málaga is not a tourist city with the attractions of Granada and Seville. Many people think of it only as a transit point to Torremolinos and Marbella, the beach paradises. But there is beauty there waiting to be discovered.

Plate 97 MÁLAGA BARRIO

This woman has never had a debate with an architect over the best place for the laundry room—whether it should be in the bedroom area where most of the dirty clothes come from, or near the kitchen where the machines can be tended while meals are prepared. She would be content to have a cold water tap and a washtub and a scrub board outside her back door. She would still have to overwork her aching shoulders and rub her fingers sore and she would still have to hang up clothes to dry. But she wouldn't have to haul a large bundle of laundry and two pails down the hill to the stream and cart the heavy wet things back again.

It is unusual to see her out in the midday sun. You would expect her to perform such chores in the coolness of the early morning, and then she would not have to work alone. In Spain, clothes-smacking on the rocks is not a solitary activity but rather a social event. Often there is a communal washhouse through which a stream is directed with convenient hip-level scrub boards. Listening to the good-natured bantering, the giggling and gossipy conversation that goes on, one almost feels sorry for the isolated suburbanite standing there pushing buttons.

Plate 98. NOONDAY, ANDALUSIA

Plate 99. WOMEN WASHING—Comonfort, Mexico

This painting was in a one-man show I once had and it was pictured in a brochure that was sent out. We received a letter back from someone saying, "I would like to order the washing picture but without the woman in the red skirt. Red does not harmonize with the colors in my living room."

One Christmas vacation we were driving around central Mexico when we came upon this scene. It was quite cold, sweater weather as you can see from the ladies in the painting; but there they were, waist-deep in the water, washing clothes. The stream was fed by hot springs. They were washing, talking, yelling, joking, and when they had finished they began to strip off their own garments down to the slip and wash those clothes, too.

Rural Mexico is still a bit on the prim side. Note the interested spectator in the distance.

Plate 100. HOT SPRINGS

Plate 101. MULE IN THE RAIN

Often when I see a rainy scene, I am struck by what I imagine it to be in sunlight. But sometimes the rain itself provides the feeling and the charm. This is such a scene. Here is a dejected mule with his drab blanket. He wishes he were back in his dry stall. With the cheerfulness of sunlight, gone would be the sad, gray mood, gone would be the wet texture of the mud, and gone too would be the plaid blanket so necessary to my design.

This painting was resting on the floor in my studio facing the wall, rejected. I had been working very hard to finish a group of paintings for a one-man show and had sent them off to the gallery. The day before the opening they called saying they needed one more picture to fill a blank space and did I have one. I said no.

Mary asked: "Where is the little church painting?"

I said: "It's facing the wall. It isn't good enough—it lacks something."

She said: "Add something."

I said: "What?"

She said: "A figure by the door."

I said: "How about a little child?"

She said: "Good idea. Why not use Elizabeth?"

Thus did Elizabeth join her mother in the ranks of stand-in models. An artist is often the poorest judge of his own work or of its possibilities. The picture was the hit of the show.

Plate 102. THE CANDLE SELLER

Plate 103. LA GRANJA

◄ The road from Málaga, Spain, to Ronda is tortuous. In the pouring rain and tired from flying all the way from New Mexico, my degree of concentration permitted attention only to the driving. I was not looking to find a scene to paint when, suddenly, around a corner, one found me. It was a farmhouse which, in Spanish, is called a "granja." Probably what struck me first about the scene was the variety of levels, then the curving of the road, the sloping paths, the olive groves in the valley and the blue hills in the distance. I needed only to turn on the sunlight to pull it all together. Ronda was still two hours away and I was dead tired and I expected never to be back, but from force of habit I took a few drab photos.

Early the next morning the sun was out, the air was crisp, the lost luggage had arrived, and my thoughts turned to "La Granja." I was rested and the four-hour round trip didn't seem so formidable. I drove to the farmhouse, presented myself to the mistress, and obtained permission to take pictures and make sketches. The sun was striking the house at just the angle I wanted. Clouds were racing across the sky, dragging their shadows over the hills. A mobile Quonset hut of a car passed by. A woman came out and began washing clothes, and finally her husband rode his horse through the center of my future painting on his way to lunch.

Everything I needed was there. Back in my studio a few weeks later, the picture almost painted itself. I had merely to rearrange some of the hills and trees and alter the architecture of the house a bit to improve the design.

A composition set on a level plane is difficult to make interesting and should be avoided unless the material is good enough to justify it. Most markets are set on level ground to facilitate the maneuvering of vehicles. All water scenes are level. This scene was designed level to focus attention on the sky and to emphasize the feeling of distance. Some small liberties were taken with the depth of the dip and the height of the mesa. ►

Plate 104. HEXAGONAL BARNS

Plate 105. BELOW RONDA

This picture, composed on different levels, is a side view of the town of Ronda. Only a few houses of the town are visible, perched on the edge of a cliff. They are the nice houses of substantial citizens. Way down below is a shantytown of rude shacks made from scavenged materials, and a few steps down from them is a stream.

Ronda is built on a mesa and one can easily see the protection it offered in ancient times against marauders. To me it offered a fine composition.

The signs on the posts warn against trespassing. What little the people have they mean to keep—including their right to privacy.

Occasionally, an artist comes across interesting figures that he wants to put into a painting except that they are arranged like birds on a wire. This is dull. Something can be done, however. For instance, this chairmaker was sitting in front of his house which was in front of another house. Everything was lined up in a row as though resting on a platform. To relieve the boredom, I introduced a slope, placing the rear house higher in the picture and slanting the ground toward the right foreground. Of course, some minor redrawing was required to adjust the perspective.

This kind of redrawing is child's play compared to some of the major reconstruction jobs that used to be required of artists in the heyday of magazine and book illustration. When, for instance, the only available reference picture of a certain type of carriage was one taken from below and the composition required a look-down angle, a detailed knowledge of carriages and a mastery of the rules of perspective were needed to save the day.

Plate 106. THE CHAIRMAKER

The burro is standing patiently, dead still, in the hot bright sunlight with only his nose tucked into the shadow. Not a stirring of wind, not a sound. The serenity is broken by the two figures, the man hauling water in his pail and the woman hanging laundry on her roof-terrace clothesline. The silence is broken by her yelling something to him.

Were it not for this unseen diagonal line of tension created between them, the picture would be dull.

Plate 107. WASHERWOMAN ON THE ROOF

Plate 108. LA ABUELA

◂ The setting for this painting is Taxco, Mexico, a town that cascades down the sides of a steep, amphitheater-shaped hill to the cathedral in its center. This vantage point, high above the dome, offers the artist an interesting perspective with a lovely view of rooftops and mountains. It offers the old lady only a long daily climb back home from the market. She has stopped to rest and chat with her granddaughter, who is doing her homework.

High in the mountains of western Spain, at the end of a narrow twisting road, lies the village of Guadalupe. It is famous for its monastery which houses a small wooden statue of the Madonna called Our Lady of Guadalupe. This very important religious relic—tradition says it was carved by St. Luke—attracts pilgrims from all over the world. Mary and I happened upon the town almost by accident and were duly impressed by the monastery, but we were really smitten by the unspoiled primitive beauty of the town itself. We stayed there for a week and I sketched several pictures. ▸

This quiet corner appealed to me and I kept returning to sketch it at different times of the day. This painting was done in afternoon light. In the morning the shadow was on the far side of the street and so were the old men. When I began working, there was a burro standing where the chicken now is. But no sooner had I begun sketching him than his owner led him up the hill and into his stall behind the two doors in the distance. I painted this large version in my studio from the sketch and from photos I had taken. I intended to include the burro but he was so strong a note that he stole attention from the rest of the painting. So he was left out.

The painting is now in the possession of good friends. When they were considering buying it, the wife's aged mother advised them not to do so because it contained no donkey. "He's known for his donkeys, you know." Hearing this, I told her there was a donkey. He was in his stall behind those doors in the back. She seemed satisfied.

The yellow bedspread dried in the sun while I was sketching and was taken in. But I kept it in my painting.

Plate 109. THE YELLOW BEDSPREAD

Plate 110. THE GREEN WATERING CAN

I was interested in the way the light reflected off the smooth, old, broken sidewalk tiles and passed through the green plastic can. That can is not for watering flowers. It is for sprinkling that lady's little patch of road in her constant and losing battle with dust. But no worry, the street will soon be paved. A motorbike-van will replace the burro, the laundry will be dried indoors, and I will move on.

Plate 111. THE OLIVE GROVE

We once stayed in a clifftop village on the western shore of the island of Majorca, high over the sea. It is reached by a narrow road which winds up the hills through beautiful silvery olive groves. The mottled light camouflaged this burro and cart until we were almost upon them.

Painting inside a woods or grove is a challenge. The patterns of the tree trunks and branches are confusing and the foliage takes on amorphous forms. I find it useful to concentrate on the negative shapes of the skyholes instead of the trees themselves and to try to make an interesting design of them.

Plate 112. A STUDY IN EARLY MORNING LIGHT

◄ I loved this scene and wanted to express its image on a grand scale. I should have known though, from the beginning, that the painting would turn out to be a "study" designed to work out a problem. The problem in this case was to catch the play of the very subtle colors produced when soft sunlight bounces back and forth on whitewashed buildings.

Why then, confronted with a project which obviously called for a trial-and-error approach, did I choose a large canvas? After a week, I was hopelessly mired in scumbled, overworked gray paint. So, chastened by failure, I began again on a canvas of manageable size and produced this result.

We were spending the summer on the Costa del Sol in Nerja, Spain. The scene was in a nearby village and I calculated that the sun would peak over the mountain at a very early hour. I set my alarm and virtuously arose in the dark and drove to the hills thinking I would wake the town. All that laundry had been done and the young men had already left for the fields.

This picture is a continuation of my study of the interplay of ► sunlight on white walls and brown dirt. The colors reflected into the shadows on a white wall are warm toward the earth and cool toward the sky. Warm also are the underplanes beneath the balconies and window tops. Here it is midday and the sun is overhead and intense. There is an urge to make shadows really dark, thinking that contrast denotes strong light. Not true. The power of the sunlight is measured by the strength of the light reflected in the shadows. The human eye is not a camera, its aperture changes automatically as it ranges over a scene. That is why in live vision there are no underexposed areas, as there are in photographs. The painter must paint values as the eye sees them, one by one, if he is to achieve the effect of actual light. The little boy doesn't realize he's being hustled through an intricate light pattern.

Plate 113. NOONDAY SUN

I was in Úbeda, Spain, and had been lost in concentration scouting for painting subjects when I realized that I had wandered out into the countryside. My route had described an arc and I found myself facing a panorama of the town from across a little valley. The shadows were long and the rays of the sun cast streaks of golden light over the landscape. The tired field workers leaving for home were unmindful of the extraordinary beauty that surrounded them.

Plate 114. ÚBEDA AT DUSK

Plate 115. EL GRAO

About five miles from the center of Valencia lies the grubby seaport town of El Grao. The word in English means "shore".
I stood on a pier looking west toward land, watched the lights blink on one by one, and let the sunset work its magic.

Plate 116. OFF PALACE AVENUE

This painting was done a couple of years before we moved to Santa Fe. We were making visits with the prospect of settling there. The area was still pretty much as I remembered it from the time I had lived there twenty-five years before. It was fall, and the crisp, thin air was pleasantly incensed with piñon smoke. The theatrical arc light of late afternoon was shining brilliantly on that white cottonwood tree. I think that is the moment when we decided to make the move.

That lady in black hauling water must have been, even then, a relic of bygone times. Or possibly of my imagination.

Wandering along, east of Palace Avenue, I happened upon José Antonio Vargas peeking curiously through this broken fence. He is a man now, but even as a little child he displayed the features of his conquering ancestors. Our adobe house was built by brothers named Vargas. They had learned the building crafts from their father, who also taught them honesty, industry and a pride in excellence.

Plate 117. JOSÉ ANTONIO VARGAS

Plate 118. CUYAMUNGUE

One Sunday morning in the fall, I found this scene in the Cuyamungue Valley near Sante Fe. To do the painting, I sat in a clearing in front of a house. I knocked on the door first to ask permission to set up my easel, but no one answered. So, certain I would do no harm, I began working and was almost through when a car pulled up with a man, a woman, and a load of children, home from church. I remember being pleased that the painting was far enough along to be completed at home should they run me off. No sign of that. The lady went into the house, the children went into the orchard, and the man came over to me. He watched me work for a while and finally said he would be pleased if I would stop in the house for a few minutes when I had finished. Over coffee, he thanked me for recognizing the beauty of "his" view. He, his father, and his grandfather before him had all been born in that house, and the memory of it with the view shown here was what sustained him as a prisoner of the Japanese during World War II. When I returned to the car, I found a bushel of apples which he had asked the children to pick while we were talking.

Mary and I have never sold this painting.

Not all New Mexicans are as sympathetic to artists as the apple farmer in Cuyamungue. A friend and I were once on a painting trip in Taos. We began setting up our easels on the shoulder of the highway in front of this scene. Suddenly, a burly gent with rheumy eyes and a shotgun stalked out of a small trailer home parked next to a little adobe house. He yelled at us to get off his property. "I don't want no picture paintin' 'roun' here!" My friend was a fairly burly gent himself and wasn't used to being pushed around and, besides, we weren't even on the man's property. So I expected trouble. But the man had a shotgun and we had heard rumors about a drug culture at that time, so we folded up our easels and headed off.

A couple of years later I was passing by and noticed that the trailer was gone but the trees and the adobe hut were still there, so this picture finally came into being.

Plate 119. BROKEN COTTONWOODS—Taos

Plate 120. NOVEMBER SUNLIGHT—Nambe, New Mexico

People who don't know New Mexico think of it only as arid desert covered with piñon trees. But lovely valleys boasting giant old cottonwood trees offer the artist another aspect to paint. This fork in the Nambe Valley is a favorite painting site of mine. I have painted it several times from different angles and in different seasons.

Plate 121. LOWER COLONIAS

One day I answered a ring at the front door to find an attractive young couple selling firewood. I bought their load and discovered they were living in a settlement called Lower Colonias, which is over the mountain from Santa Fe north of Pecos. Since Pecos itself is somewhat of an outpost, I was curious about Lower Colonias and began asking questions about it as a possible painting site. They invited me to pay them a visit the next day to see their logging wagon operation for myself. They warned me to put chains on the car because of deep snow and to arrive at the appointed time when they would meet me at the outskirts, since Lower Colonias natives don't take kindly to strangers.

I spent a delightful day with them and took many photographs from which I painted several pictures. This is one.

This view of Rodriguez Street in Santa Fe was done on the spot. Later I made a large painting of the same scene in my studio with a satisfactory result. But successful as a painting may be with respect to refinement, good drawing, accurate values, there is no way it can match the charming spontaneity of a quick sketch. In a sketch, statements must be made simply and fast, right or wrong, especially on a cold day. Snow is fun to paint but tricky; the values are deceptive because of the bright light. Snow pictures should, when possible, be sketched at the scene before working from a photograph back in the studio.

Here are some general rules for painting snow which I find helpful. Break them when you must, but break them knowingly: Keep the shadow pattern simple, don't overmodel. Keep the shadows lighter than you think they should be. Stay away from strong blues. Look for places in the shadows where you can use lots of warm but subtle colors. They will give your painting vitality and richness. Paint top planes in the light a warm, pale gray. Use pure white sparingly for accents and side planes.

Plate 122. RODRIGUEZ STREET

In the fall of 1967, the United States Department of the Interior, with the help of the Society of Illustrators, embarked on a project to have paintings made of all the national parks. It fell to me to paint the Grand Canyon. At that time, I had never seen the canyon which was to play such an important part in my career. I had, of course, seen many pictures of the canyon. I wanted to try to do something different, perhaps a mid-air view from a helicopter or a look-up view from Phantom Lodge at the bottom. For this reason, I asked the government to promise the use of a helicopter. This was given very reluctantly as there was at that time much pressure to keep commercial interests out of the parks. Helicopters were banned except for very special government business. Mary and I had another private reason. We were expecting a baby and the doctor had said no mule rides or four-hour hikes.

I made arrangements with the park rangers to coordinate our helicopter ride with the arrival of a pack train at a particular switchback halfway down, so that I could take pictures of the canyon from mid-air with riders and animals in the foreground. In practice, this never worked out because as we got close enough to take pictures, we were waved off. The helicopter was starting to spook the mules. Our overnight visit to Phantom Lodge on the canyon floor was also a disappointment. Before we could find our cabin, a blackout occurred. A moonless night at the bottom of the Grand Canyon during a power failure is a black night indeed. With the help of some vague directions and a box of matches we somehow found a couple of beds.

Once back on top, I spent five days exploring the South Rim from end to end, taking hundreds of photographs and learning something about the canyon itself. This painting is of the beginning of the Kaibab Trail; it is one of several that resulted from that first trip.

Plate 123. KAIBAB TRAIL, FALL

Five years after our first trip to the Grand Canyon, I was invited to participate in the first showing of a new organization called The National Academy of Western Art at The Cowboy Hall of Fame in Oklahoma City. This was to replace the annual show of the Cowboy Artists of America, which had gone elsewhere. Western art was to be redefined to include any subject matter from the seventeen western states, not just cowboys and Indians and frontier life. The show was to be a competition for gold, silver and bronze medals and a grand prize of a large sum of money and a European trip.

Without much thought of medals and money, I regarded this as a really fine opportunity to become known to this great new market for realistic art. There was never any question in my mind of what to paint. I could think of no subject that more definitively represents the West than the Grand Canyon. And how better to show it than after a fresh snowfall?

Having been told by phone that there would be snow, I flew to Flagstaff, Arizona, and drove to the canyon. No snow! But I was assured that it was on the way. While waiting, I spent my time carefully studying vantage points and planning my picture. I had painted Kaibab Trail on the South Rim on my first trip and been satisfied. I decided to try the same scene with snow. I arranged the hire of a mule skinner and mules.

After three days the snow finally came. I worked all day photographing the canyon in different lights and from different angles. It took the mules an hour to make the round trip down to a turning area and they did it over and over to give me many photos from which to compose my final picture.

My love of the Grand Canyon must have been shared by the jury at the show because the Prix de West, as that grand prize is called, was awarded to my painting.

Plate 124. KAIBAB TRAIL, WINTER

The Bright Angel trail is also on the South Rim of the Grand Canyon; it starts from the western side of a promontory and presents a different aspect from that of the Kaibab Trail.

Plate 125. BRIGHT ANGEL TRAIL

Plate 126. PACK TRAIN

This picture is about as close as I have ever come to painting traditional Western subject matter.

The string of mules and horses has just hauled five tourists up from the canyon floor.

Northwestern Connecticut is an area of great charm and beauty. There are thickets, hills, meadows, walls, white clapboard houses and red barns. There are even some donkeys, but they are pets and don't seem to have the character of their working brothers abroad. Connecticut also has gray barns and red trucks.

Plate 127. THE GRAY BARN

Plate 128. WASHINGTON MEADOW

Even on a clear fall day in Connecticut there is still a beautiful soft haze in the air that seems to go with lush grass and old walls.

I have mentioned that my admiration for Vermeer is very great. So it is inevitable that I should, from time to time, come up with a painting showing his influence. *The Acoma Potter* is such a painting.

I was searching for a subject with a theme that would be appropriate for a National Academy of Western Art Show and got the idea of painting an Indian potter at work in a setting reminiscent of those used by my Dutch idol. I happened to be discussing this over an iced tea after a tennis game with my Santa Fe friend, Carl Bibo. He said, "I'll ask my cousin, Juana Leno, to pose. She is an Acoma Indian and earns her living making pots." It developed that Carl's father, an itinerant Jewish peddler from Westphalia, Germany, had traded with the Acoma tribe thirty miles west of Albuquerque, married an Indian maiden, and settled in Acoma Pueblo. He became so beloved that he was elected Chief—the only Jewish Indian chief on record—and for two terms!

Carl made arrangements for us to visit Juana and on the appointed day we drove down to Acoma. She greeted us in her workroom, which she had cleaned and arranged with examples of her pots on a table. She herself was very nattily dressed, as if she were going shopping in the city. The "workroom" was her kitchen, complete with new linoleum flooring, modern stove, refrigerator, washer, dryer, etc. With what I hoped was tact, I explained that I wanted to record something a bit more traditional, even historical, and that I needed a rustic setting. What did she think? "Well," she replied, "why don't we go down to my old workroom that I was using until just a month ago? But you probably won't like it." I loved it! I was able to plan and paint this picture. I didn't have the heart to ask her to put on work clothes, but luckily prudence required that she change her shoes and don an apron before going down to the little old hut.

As the work of setting up my picture progressed, I became more and more impressed with her pots, so I placed an order to buy one and made an appointment to return for it in a month. What I saw when I went back has caused me never to complain again about having to discard an unsatisfactory painting after much effort. Acoma pots are intricately decorated with a one-hair brush and are as thin as egg shells. Each one represents many hours of careful work. For firing, they are gently packed in a hole in the ground and left for several days under a carefully tended covering of smoldering animal dung. It is a most delicate and painstaking process. If a pot is not perfectly formed, or if the firing heat is uneven, cracking results. Juana Leno waited until my arrival before uncovering the four pots she had been firing. She gingerly brushed away the ashes. The pots were all broken!

Plate 129. THE ACOMA POTTER

Plate 130. THE KACHINA DOLL MAKER

Plate 131. THE KACHINA DOLL MAKER (sketch)

This painting was inspired by one called *The Mask Maker*, by the Russian artist Abram Arkhipov. In 1974, Mary and I spent some time in Leningrad and Moscow, where I discovered the work of many wonderful realist painters I had never heard of. At that time few paintings by these artists had been widely reproduced, even in Russia, and the only records of them I could bring home were the few slide photos I was permitted to take. The use of flash, even tripods, was forbidden in museums. The light was dim and most of the paintings were covered with glass. This meant exposures of up to a second with a hand-held camera, so that most of my slides are fuzzy images of the paintings seen through reflections of myself. The ones of *The Mask Maker* were good enough to refresh my memory of that fine painting. In my mind there seemed to be a kinship between makers of Russian theatrical masks and makers of Hopi Indian Kachina dolls. I had a challenge—to find the right model. This time I was not as fortunate as I had been with *The Acoma Potter*.

One day, after several months of asking around, a friend suggested that I attend the annual Indian Arts and Crafts Show in Santa Fe. I introduced myself to George Pooley, the son of Emil Pooley, reputed to be the finest Hopi Kachina doll maker. I persuaded George and his wife to come to my studio to see my work and to hear about my project. I showed him this oil sketch of the proposed painting which I had done from my imagination. George was sympathetic to my idea. He loved his father and revered him as an artist and wanted him to be painted for posterity. However, his father was undergoing weekly medical treatments and was quite ill. George said he would let me know when it would be possible for the old gentleman to pose. About six months later I received a call asking me to go to their home near Window Rock, Arizona. I was to be allotted only an hour of his time.

I spent most of the hour arranging the still life objects used in doll making and readying my camera and the floodlamps. Mr. Pooley appeared, very frail, in a flowered shirt. I asked if it could be changed because I didn't want its design to distract from his dolls.

I painted my picture and shortly afterward Emil Pooley died. He was a gentle man with a fine talent. I am glad to see that his dolls are being increasingly appreciated as works of art. I am glad, also, that the present owners of my painting have been for years personal friends and admirers of Emil Pooley.

Plate 132. THE JUNGFRAU

Switzerland is a great place to paint. Its people are polite and considerate of artists, and there is a wide choice of painting subjects to satisfy any taste or mood. There are picturesque old cities like Lausanne, Basel and Lucerne. There are lovely lakes like Leman and Lugano. There are quaint domestic farm scenes where they still employ oxen and horses. There is German, French and Italian architecture available, depending on the region, and there is spectacular mountain scenery. This painting was made almost thirty years ago on the easel shown in the photograph.

Plate 133. CERISE

    Once Mary and I stayed for a few days in the southern Swiss city of Sion. From there five or six deep narrow valleys fan out, dotted with tiny settlements like this one which is called Cerise. There were majestic mountains stationed behind those clouds and they revealed themselves periodically while I was doing the field sketch for this painting. I chose in the end to cover them with mist because they stole interest from my hillside village.

Plate 134. GIRL WATERING HER BURRO

While the child in *The Candle Seller* was actually modeled by Elizabeth, the one in *Girl Watering Her Burro* was not. I was in Portugal gathering material on one of those twelve-day, get-away package tours, having left Mary and Elizabeth at home. It was our first separation for even a night and I was feeling very lonely and homesick. I came across this little girl, just Elizabeth's age, and was very close to chucking the get-away package and flying home. Only my pressing need for material kept me there.

My parents moved to Baton Rouge when I was a teen-ager, and I considered it a second home during all my bachelor years. When I lived there painting portraits, I had occasion to travel around the southern part of Louisiana many times and I fell under its spell. Those were the days before the onslaught of progress after World War II, when life was still relaxed and gracious, reminiscent of the culture of the French and English planters who had settled there a hundred and fifty years before.

Once I stayed at Afton Villa for several weeks, painting five family portraits. It was a lovely French style ante-bellum mansion, set among gorgeous azalea gardens and giant live oak trees dripping with Spanish moss. James Audubon once lived there as an itinerant portrait painter and dancing instructor. Afton Villa has since been destroyed by fire, as have so many other plantation homes. I sketched Afton, I sketched The Cottage (only twenty rooms), I sketched Greenwood—all now gone. The pull of nostalgia for the recent past, a century or so ago, is very strong. Many people lament the destruction of its remnants. But some are doing something to preserve them. Greenwood plantation house has been magnificently reconstructed from original plans, as have Afton Villa's gardens.

Plate 135. AFTON VILLA

Plate 136. GREENWOOD

Today the beautiful Spanish moss which gave the Louisiana landscape its mood of softness and mystery is gone. It is a plant which feeds on the air, and in Louisiana the air has been poisoned by the fumes spewed out by chemical plants which now line the Mississippi River. They say that when the pollution is cleared up, as it inevitably will be, the moss will come back.

This man made his living gathering and selling the Spanish moss. Its soft gray covering was removed and the springy hair inside was used as mattress filling. I wonder what he does now?

Plate 137. SPANISH MOSS GATHERER

Gone are the little cabins built on stilts in the swamps of Louisiana. They were all swept away by Hurricane Audrey in 1957, and have been replaced by houseboats which can rise and fall with a tidal wave. Gone too are the pirogue dugout canoes propelled like gondolas—now there are motor boats.

Plate 138. PIERRE PART

Plate 139. WINDRUSH PLANTATION COTTAGE

One man has devoted his life to collecting the artifacts of Southern plantation life, ranging from kitchen implements to slave cabins. He has built the Rural Life Museum which is located on his own family's Windrush Plantation in Baton Rouge. We are fortunate to have people with such ingenuity, taste and intelligence, as well as a strong collector's urge.

This cottage was on the original plantation and is now part of the museum.

The intrusion of industry need not always be bad. While wandering around the canals in the swamp area west of Baton Rouge, I watched this lady and her companion, around the bend nearby, fishing. I was there painting all day and I never saw them catch a fish, but I saw them periodically visit a giant new Cadillac automobile and extract a beer from an ice chest in the trunk. That house across the street is actually a barbershop, and the barber told me the story of these two women.

They were sisters who lived on a little patch of land which had been deeded to their grandfather when he was freed after the Civil War. Recently oil had been struck there, and they were paid a lump sum (the Cadillac) and a small monthly stipend for their share of the oil taken from the pool under the area.

They quit tending their truck garden and they quit their menial jobs. From then on, they fished. They had prestige (the Cadillac) and leisure, and they lived within their means in their own world. Seldom has "easy-come" money been so wisely used.

Plate 140. LOUISIANA FISHERWOMAN

Plate 141. OLD MANOR HOUSE BY THE SEA

This old house on the Connemara in Ireland has withstood centuries of storms from the Atlantic. The first two-man team to fly the ocean barely made it to a spot just west of here. That bird is flying directly away from us toward Long Island.

I have said before that I am a painter of the trial-and-error method. Rather than plan carefully with many drawings and color sketches, I put an initial statement on canvas, and then make change after change until I am satisfied that I cannot improve it. Sometimes the changes are in values, and I adjust them back and forth to achieve a certain light effect. Sometimes they are in degrees of detail to produce emphasis or to eliminate a worked-over look. When painting in Ireland, the changes are invariably in color. The exercise is in toning down the greens (they don't call it The Emerald Isle for nothing). The intensity of that color is extreme. But what is rich and beautiful in nature can be cheap and garish in paint. And in Ireland one must resist temptation and keep the dull greens handy. While I was painting the five pictures shown on these pages, there was a struggle as I added more and more olives and grays, until in the end only a few discriminating flecks of pure pigment were left on a blanket of lesser greens. With color, so much can be suggested with so little.

Most of the cottage roofs in Ireland today are slate or composition shingle. Thatched roofs are quite rare, so when I saw a man walking beside a donkey cart laden with straw, I followed him to his destination—this scene. He and another old man had a negotiating session over the load of straw. There was plenty of mock-angry Gaelic exchanged before a bargain was struck, whereupon the load was dumped, ready to be used to patch the roof.

Plate 142. THATCH DELIVERY

Plate 143. EMPTY CART

Plate 144. EMPTY CART (detail)

The load of thatch has been left, the men and their dogs have bid each other farewell, and the donkey with the cart is led away.

The actual-size reproduction is included not only to show the painting technique and surface texture, but also as proof that the stamp of Ireland can be seen on a face as well as on a landscape.

Plate 145. BEFORE THE IRISH WIND

The name of this man is Val Coneeley. He is a potato farmer in the community of Balley Coneeley and he lives alone. He feeds himself with some of the potatoes he grows. He earns a small income selling the rest. He warms himself with the peat he digs and brings home using this donkey and wagon. Home is the thatched cottage in the distance.

I struck up an acquaintance with him while painting the sketch shown here. I watched him dig potatoes and haul peat. He was very much interested in my work and posed for me graciously. Though he is poor, he refused the ten pounds I offered him for this service. He finally took it when I pointed out that he need not keep it for himself. He could buy ale at the pub for all his friends.

Many years later, as an adult and as an artist traveling in Spain, Italy, Mexico and the Middle East where burros abound, I found myself attracted to them and wanting to paint them. They appeal so much to my plebeian taste.

Burros have long ears, stocky shaggy shapes, and large hung-down humble heads—not at all graceful, sleek, and arrogant like race horses and leopards and other animals. But they have a dignity about them.

They are very strong—probably pound for pound the strongest mammal—but they do not misuse their strength. They seem willing to take unlimited abuse rather than comply with an order they choose not to obey. They cannot be hurried. They will not be backed up if they cannot see where they're going (rare intelligence, not stubbornness). They are sturdy. Their thick hide protects them from insects and disease. They can eat almost anything and can go for long periods without water.

I would like to finish my gallery of paintings with a small group of some of my burro friends. People often ask me the difference between a burro and a donkey. There is none. The Spanish word "burro" has gained common English usage, so the words have become interchangeable.

As I have mentioned already, I believe a lifelong choice of subject matter for an artist somehow traces back to childhood influences. My love affair with the burro probably began when, as a child in Spain, I was taken often to visit the home of our maid Maria. Her family owned a small burro which was used occasionally as a beast of light burden but was primarily a pet—a gentle, nuzzling pet that followed us around and gave us rides.

Plate 146. VAL CONEELEY'S HOUSE (sketch)

Plate 147. BURRO PULLING LOGS AT ASWAN

Plate 148. OLD MAN GOING HOME

If left to their own devices and their own pace, they will serve well. They are by nature sure-footed, loyal and affectionate.

Plate 149. FLOWER BURRO

Plate 150. BOY FILLING WATER CANS

Plate 151. BOY LEADING WATER BURRO

They have the calmness and gentleness of those who fear nothing. But they will bray to warn others of genuine danger.
They are wonderful models because they stand still for hours.

Plate 152. SANTA FE FESTIVAL POSTER BURRO

Plate 153. TWO BURROS IN AN ALLEY

They can be trusted. ►

Plate 154. THE BABY SITTER

Plate 155. BROWN MULE

BIOGRAPHY

Photograph by Don Blair

Clark Hulings was born in 1922 in Florida where his father Courtland M. Hulings was manager of a plant that produced a gas for fumigating orange trees. Clark's mother, Anner Everett Hulings, died of tuberculosis when he was an infant and he and his sister Susan lived with their maternal grandparents for the next three years.

During this time Clark's father was transferred to Valencia, Spain. While there he became intrigued with paintings by Spanish artists of local scenes in the brilliant light and he purchased several of them. Mr. Hulings met and married the daughter of the British Consul in Valencia and soon Clark and his sister joined them.

Those early years in the colorful sunny atmosphere of Spain left lasting impressions which are still evident in Clark's work.

In 1928 the Hulings returned to the United States and settled in Westfield, New Jersey. Clark was in the first grade when he painted a recognizable pastel portrait of his step-mother. This was the earliest indication of his special inclination for art. As a teenager, Clark acquired a small box of oil paints and brushes and began to copy many of the paintings that his father had collected in Spain, as well as a postcard reproduction of *The Calmady Children* by Sir Thomas Lawrence, a painting which he had seen at the Metropolitan Museum of Art. The copies were good, his father was duly impressed, and art lessons were arranged. The teacher, Sigmund Ivanowski, was a fine portrait and landscape painter who had studied at the St. Petersburg Academy in Russia around the turn of the century. He impressed upon young Hulings the need to master basic skills, particularly drawing.

By the time Clark graduated from high school, his health was fragile and he was unable to enter college. However, he continued a limited schedule of study with Ivanowski as well as with George Bridgman, the celebrated drawing teacher at The Art Students' League in New York City. In the fall of 1941 Clark enrolled in Haverford College, and in response to his father's concern that he study for a "practical" career he majored in physics. After his graduation in 1944 he was headed for an appointment to work on the "Manhatten Project" in Los Alamos, New Mexico. However, his recurring ill health denied him acceptance for the job. Recuperating in Santa Fe, he began to sketch and paint again to fill the empty hours.

Before long he was supporting himself, painting pastel portraits of children. In the spring of 1945 he had a one-man show of his landscapes at the New Mexico Art Museum in Santa Fe. Shortly thereafter he went to work in a laboratory in Denver, Colorado. Every week he spent his day off in the mountains painting landscapes and his evenings in drawing classes at Denver University.

In 1946, while visiting his parents in Louisiana, he was invited to mount a one-man show of his work at the galleries of the Louisiana Art Commission. He included several portraits of family members. This show launched him on a successful career as a portrait painter.

During this period he continued to paint landscapes and also became interested in illustration and design. In 1948 such interest took him back to New York City and the Art Student's League—this time to study with Frank Reilly, noted illustrator and teacher.

He worked intensely for three years, and in 1951 he gained employment in an art studio doing wash drawings of hams, turkeys and holiday decorations for a newspaper mat agency that specialized in ads for supermarkets. In his spare time he produced samples with which to solicit work as a free-lance painter of covers for paperback books and record albums and illustrations for adventure magazines. This business was demanding. To be successful, it was necessary to become versatile in technique, media and subject matter. One had to work well from all kinds of reference material as well as from imagination and to design around type areas and page shapes. Also, one had to learn to simplify and to exaggerate to produce an immediate impact and to accommodate the limitations of reproduction. The rigid deadlines of the publishing business developed working habits and self-discipline which have been useful to Hulings ever since.

The struggle of those years of school and commercial illustration was supported by frequent visits to Louisiana to execute portrait commissions. By 1956 Hulings' career as an illustrator was firmly established. But the constant lure of landscape painting sent him on a visit to Europe. This happy time was spent wandering through picture galleries and painting out in the open. Approaching winter forced him further and further south—all the way to Sicily, where he rediscovered sun-baked villages and donkeys.

After four months, conscience and duty called him back to his New York work. But the call was not very strong, and less than two years later he packed up again and went back to Europe—this time for a stay which lasted three years.

From these travels Hulings returned with hundreds of small pen and water color sketches and countless photographs. These sketches and photographs formed the nucleus of the large collection of pictures which still provides reference material for his paintings.

In the fall of 1960 he returned to New York City and resumed his illustration career to recoup finances, but this time he planned his work schedule to include serious easel painting. His paintings began to sell, and within two years this new pursuit became not only more satisfying but economically more profitable than illustration, and he decided to devote all his attention to it. He began placing his work in competitive shows of realistic art and won several awards, the most prized being The Council of American Artists Award at the Hudson Valley Art Association for *Restaurante Vicente* (Plate 4) and the gold medal given by The Allied Artists of America for his painting *Onteniente* (Plate 10).

In 1967 members of The Society of Illustrators were invited by the Department of the Interior to paint scenes of this country's national parks. Clark painted the Grand Canyon. This was to be the first of six paintings he has done of that magnificent scene. One of those, *The Grand Canyon, Kaibab Trail* (Plate 124), won the coveted Prix de West at the initial show in 1973 of The National Academy of Western Art in Oklahoma City. He went on to win three silver and two gold medals for both oil and water color at subsequent competitions at NAWA.

In 1976 *A Collection of Oil Paintings by Clark Hulings* was published by The Lowell Press as a catalog accompanying a one-man show held under the auspices of The National Academy of Western Art. He was presented with the Hall's Trustees' gold medal for his "distinguished contribution to American art."

In 1980 Clark's painting *The Pink Parasol* (Plate 87), won wide acclaim at the annual Western Heritage Auction Sale in Houston, Texas. *Kaleidoscope,* (Plate 75) the oil submitted in the 1981 Sale, repeated the triumph and brought another record price.

Clark married Mary Belfi in 1966 and their daughter Elizabeth was born two years later. When they are not traveling, they live in Santa Fe.

1. EL MERCADO CENTRAL—Valencia
   Oil   20"x30"
   Mr. & Mrs. George Harris

2. EL MERCADO CENTRAL—Valencia
   Detail—actual size

3. THE SCAVENGERS
   Oil   9"x11"
   John and Gloria Silver

4. RESTAURANTE VICENTE—Saler
   Oil   32"x46"
   Collection of the artist

5. RESTAURANTE VICENTE—Saler
   Detail—actual size

6. THE RED RAINCOAT—Valencia
   Oil   28"x48"
   Mrs. John W. Starr

7. ILE DE LA CITÉ—Paris
   Oil   28"x42"
   Mr. & Mrs. John L. Hendry III

8. OLD LADY IN BLACK—Valencia
   Oil   30"x46"
   Private collection

9. CONVERSATION
   Oil   20"x30"
   Mr. & Mrs. Michael Halebian

10. ONTENIENTE
    Oil   20"x48"
    Collection of the artist

11. ONTENIENTE Detail—actual size

12. GRANADA PRODUCE STALL
    Oil   18"x27"
    Mr. Norman F. Jones

13. GRANADA PLAZA
    Oil   30"x42"
    Mr. & Mrs. Rollin King

14. MULES OF TARANCÓN, STANDING
    Oil   20"x30"
    Private collection

15. MULES OF TARANCÓN, RUNNING
    Oil   20"x30"
    Private collection

16. TORREMOLINOS AT DAWN
    Oil   10"x20"
    Mr. & Mrs. Howard W. Parker

17. CASA SUECIA (Swedish House)
    Oil   20"x24"
    Private collection

18. ALTEA Detail of girl—actual size

19. ALTEA
    Oil   34"x21"
    Mrs. Donald L. Brown

20. ALTEA Detail of wall—actual size

21. THE GIRL AND THE CAT
    Oil   16"x20"
    Elizabeth Hulings

22. FAMILY PORTRAIT
    Oil   16"x24"
    Mr. James R. Cox

23. THAT GREEK TREE PICTURE
    Oil   24"x36"
    Collection of the artist

24. GREEK WOMEN WASHING
    Oil   24"x36"
    Private collection

25. WHITE ROSES WITH ONION
    Oil   16"x12"
    Elizabeth Hulings

26. BACKLIT ROSE
    Oil   12"x12"
    Mr. & Mrs. Bobby Holt

27. CHRYSANTHEMUMS
    Oil   20"x24"
    Private collection

28. THE SPIRIT LAMP
    Oil   20"x20"
    Paul and Doris Masa

29. STILL LIFE WITH VIOLETS
    Oil   25"x30"
    Mrs. Virginia Mullin

30. MARY, ELIZABETH AND PAULINE
    Oil   45"x45"
    Collection of the artist

31. ELIZABETH, BABY
    Oil   11"x10"
    Collection of the artist

32. ELIZABETH, 1½ YEARS
    Oil   11"x10"
    Collection of the artist

33. ELIZABETH AND FEATHER, 8 YEARS
    Oil   5½"x8"
    Collection of the artist

34. ELIZABETH, 12 YEARS
    Oil   14"x12"
    Collection of the artist

35. THE SPANISH SHAWL
    Oil   30"x20"
    Mrs. Virginia Mullin

36. SAN JOSÉ MISSION
    Watercolor   30"x20"
    Mr. & Mrs. John L. Hendry III

37. WATERCOLOR ROSES
    Watercolor   16"x12"
    Mary Hulings

38. CHURCH AT TRAMPAS, NEW MEXICO
    Watercolor   16"x24"
    Mary Hulings

39. INDIAN MARKET
    Watercolor   12"x16"
    Mr. & Mrs. Frank Crane

40. MAN OF PLAV
    Watercolor   17"x14"
    Mr. & Mrs. Andrew Belfi

41. EGYPTIANS
    Watercolor   9"x11"
    Private collection

42. KONYA MOSQUE
    Watercolor   13½"x17½"
    Private collection

43. CHURCH—Rieka, Yugoslavia
    Watercolor   19"x14"
    Private collection

44. PARIS VIGNETTE
    Watercolor   14"x17"
    Private collection

45. YUGOSLAVIAN STREET PHOTOGRAPHER
    Oil   12"x16"
    Collection of the artist

46. LITTLE CHAPEL AT DUBROVNIK
    Watercolor   12"x14"
    Private collection

47. DUBROVNIK CATHEDRAL
    Watercolor   14"x12"
    Mr. & Mrs. Harry Ottinger

48. MARKET SCENE I—Skopje
Watercolor 15"x20"
Collection of the artist

49. MARKET SCENE II—Skopje
Watercolor 15"x20"
Collection of the artist

50. OUTSKIRTS OF THE SKOPJE MARKET
Oil 24"x36"
Private collection

51. COVERED POOL—Istanbul
Watercolor 14½"x19"
Ms. Rita Merkert

52. CARRIAGE TAXI—Konya, Turkey
Oil 20"x30"
Private collection

53. QUARRY CART—Mersin, Turkey
Oil 22"x28"
The Arizona Bank

54. TEMPLE OF KARNAK—Luxor
Watercolor 11"x15½"
Private collection

55. LUXOR FERRYBOAT
Oil 24"x36"
Mary Hulings

56. CAIRO RUG MERCHANT
Oil 18"x12"
Mr. & Mrs. John L. Hendry III

57. THE LONELY MAN
Oil 20"x30"
Private collection

58. RAINY STREET—Sicily
Oil 24"x30"
Collection of the artist

59. RANDAZZO—Sicily
Oil 25"x50"
Mr. & Mrs. W. F. Roden

60. STREET IN NAPLES
Oil 20"x8"
Private collection

61. SUZY
Oil 16"x12"
Collection of the artist

62. NANCY
Oil 20"x30"
Mrs. John W. Kieckhefer

63. SARA
Oil 27"x18"
Carol and Jules Green

64. SYLVIA
Oil 16"x20"
Private collection

65. A ROOFTOP VIEW OF ARGENTAT
Oil 27"x44"
Mr. & Mrs. John L. Hendry III

66. FEEDING THE CHICKENS
Oil 22"x32"
Mr. & Mrs. Alex Halff

67. VILLE FRANCHE
Oil 30"x42"
Mr. & Mrs. James S. Fowler

68. THE RED SWING—Brantôme
Oil 24"x48"
Mr. & Mrs. T. Boone Pickens

69. HIERSAC CHÂTEAU
Oil 19"x34"
Mr. & Mrs. George A. Thomas

70. HIERSAC CHÂTEAU—(sketch, first visit)
Oil 8"x12"
Mrs. John W. Starr

71. HIERSAC CHÂTEAU—(sketch, second visit)
Oil 8"x16"
Mr. & Mrs. J. Pfifer Lewis

72. CLOTH VENDORS—San Miguel de Allende
Oil 24"x36"
Mr. & Mrs. Michael Halebian

73. THE PINK SERAPE
Oil 18"x30"
Mr. & Mrs. Ken Johns

74. THE LOWER MARKET
Oil 34"x42"
Private collection

75. KALEIDOSCOPE
Oil 29"x46"
Private collection

76. KALEIDOSCOPE Detail of figures—actual size

77. KALEIDOSCOPE Detail of head—actual size

78. THE MEXICAN ROSARY MAN
Oil 16"x20"
Mr. James R. Cox

79. WINDY MARKET DAY
Oil 32"x46"
Mr. & Mrs. Joseph I. O'Neill

80. THE MELON STAND
Oil 20"x30"
Mr. & Mrs. Robert M. Eagle

81. CHAPALA FRUIT VENDOR
Oil 18"x27"
Collection of the Artist

82. THE GUARDIAN
Oil 24"x36"
Private collection

83. BURRO ALLEY, SANTA FE, 1900
Oil 30"x50"
Museum of the Southwest—Midland, Texas

84. ASINO ALLEY—Taormina
Oil 8"x10"
Private collection

85. SAN MIGUEL WOOD MERCHANT
Oil 22"x33"
Private collection

86. CHICHICASTENANGO—Guatemala
Oil 40"x40"
Mr. & Mrs. John L. Hendry III

87. THE PINK PARASOL
Oil 32"x46"
Mr. & Mrs. John F. Eulich

88. THE PLASTIC BAG LADY
Oil 12"x18"
Mr. & Mrs. Charles Dean

89. AFTERNOON BUS
Oil 19"x29"
Mr. & Mrs. John L. Hendry III

90. VELEZ MÁLAGA COURTYARD
Oil 22"x33"
Mr. & Mrs. Russell J. Ramsland

91. SALTILLO—Mexico
Oil 20"x30"
Mr. & Mrs. Snuff Garrett

92. TIMELESS ADOBE (sketch)
Oil 14"x21"
Private collection

93. TIMELESS ADOBE
Oil 32"x46"
Mr. & Mrs. John R. McCune

94. WOODBEARERS OF CHIMAYO
Oil 30"x60"
Mr. & Mrs. Wilbur Zink

95. LOUISIANA CABIN
Oil 20"x30"
Private collection

96. TAXCO HORSEMAN
Oil 24"x36"
Private collection

97. MÁLAGA BARRIO
Oil 22"x32"
Mr. & Mrs. Bobby Holt

98. NOONDAY, ANDALUSIA
Oil 28"x42"
Mr. & Mrs. Thurmond A. Williamson

99. MONDAY MORNING—Comonfort
Oil 29"x32"
Mr. & Mrs. William B. Lloyd

100. HOT SPRINGS
Oil 24"x36"
Mr. & Mrs. William P. Clements, Jr.

101. MULE IN THE RAIN (detail)
Oil 12"x15"
Private collection

102. THE CANDLE SELLER
Oil 22"x33"
Private collection

103. LA GRANJA
Oil 24"x36"
Mr. & Mrs. Wayne Rumley

104. HEXAGONAL BARNS
Oil 25"x30"
Private collection

105. BELOW RONDA
Oil 30"x36"
Mr. & Mrs. Donald Hansen

106. THE CHAIRMAKER
Oil 18"x36"
Mr. & Mrs. James S. Fowler

107. WASHERWOMAN ON THE ROOF
Oil 24"x36"
Private collection

108. LA ABUELA
Oil 28"x42"
Private collection

109. THE YELLOW BEDSPREAD
Oil 29"x32"
Mr. & Mrs. Frank Crane

110. THE GREEN WATERING CAN
Oil 30"x20"
Mr. George Montgomery

111. THE OLIVE GROVE
Oil 12"x18"
Private collection

112. A STUDY IN EARLY MORNING LIGHT
Oil 20"x16"
Private collection

113. NOONDAY SUN
Oil 18"x20"
Mrs. John W. Starr

114. ÚBEDA AT DUSK
Oil 30"x45"
Mr. & Mrs. Robert O'Neill

115. EL GRAO
Oil 20"x28"
Private collection

116. OFF PALACE AVENUE
Oil 20"x30"
Mr. & Mrs. William E. Reardon

117. JOSÉ ANTONIO VARGAS
Oil 16"x24"
Mr. & Mrs. J. Pfifer Lewis

118. CUYAMUNGUE
Oil 12"x18"
Mary Hulings

119. BROKEN COTTONWOODS—Taos
Oil 16"x24"
Mr. & Mrs. William C. Whitridge

120. NOVEMBER SUNLIGHT—Nambe, New Mexico
Oil 29"x48"
Private collection

121. LOWER COLONIAS—New Mexico
Oil 24"x36"
Mr. & Mrs. Bob Duke

122. RODRIGUEZ STREET
Oil 12"x16"
Mr. & Mrs. Elliott Phillips

123. KAIBAB TRAIL, FALL
Oil 32"x46"
Private collection

124. KAIBAB TRAIL, WINTER
Oil 27"x54"
National Cowboy Hall of Fame

125. BRIGHT ANGEL TRAIL
Oil 24"x36"
Mr. & Mrs. James S. Fowler

126. PACK TRAIN
Oil 22"x33"
Private collection

127. THE GRAY BARN
Oil 32"x46"
Private collection

128. WASHINGTON MEADOW
Oil 28"x42"
Private collection

129. THE ACOMA POTTER
Oil 24"x30"
Mr. & Mrs. James S. Fowler

130. THE KACHINA DOLL MAKER
Oil 28"x36"
Mr. & Mrs. Donald Hansen

131. THE KACHINA DOLL MAKER (sketch)
Oil 12"x14"
Collection of the artist

132. THE JUNGFRAU
Oil 20"x26"
Mr. & Mrs. Richard Cadwallader

133. CERISE
Oil 28"x44"
Mr. & Mrs. James Shelton

134. GIRL WATERING HER BURRO
Oil 20"x30"
Mr. & Mrs. Robert Anderson

135. AFTON VILLA
Pencil 10"x12"
Private collection

136. GREENWOOD
Pencil 10"x12"
Private collection

137. SPANISH MOSS GATHERER
Oil 21"x34"
Mr. & Mrs. Clifford Ourso

138. PIERRE PART
Oil 21"x34"
Mr. & Mrs. Drew Mayfield

139. WINDRUSH PLANTATION COTTAGE
    Oil 24"x36"
    Mrs. Vinita Wiederkehr

140. LOUISIANA FISHERWOMAN
    Oil 22"x33"
    Private collection

141. OLD MANOR HOUSE BY THE SEA
    Oil 12"x16"
    Private collection

142. THATCH DELIVERY
    Oil 21"x35"
    Private collection

143. EMPTY CART
    Oil 21"x35"
    Collection of the artist

144. EMPTY CART
    Detail—
    actual size

145. BEFORE THE IRISH WIND
    Oil 24"x36"
    Mr. & Mrs. Charles S. Pearce

146. VAL CONEELEY'S HOUSE
    Oil 12"x16"
    Collection of the artist

147. BURRO PULLING LOGS AT ASWAN
    Oil 16"x30"
    Private collection

148. OLD MAN GOING HOME
    Oil 12"x18"
    Mr. & Mrs. J. Pfifer Lewis

149. FLOWER BURRO
    Oil 12"x12"
    Elizabeth Hulings

150. BOY FILLING WATER CANS
    Oil 14"x12"
    Mr. & Mrs. John L. Hendry III

151. BOY LEADING WATER BURRO
    Oil 12"x14"
    Private collection

152. SANTA FE FESTIVAL POSTER BURRO
    Oil 12"x18"
    Elizabeth Hulings

153. TWO BURROS IN AN ALLEY
    Oil 14"x21"
    Private collection

154. THE BABY SITTER
    Oil 20"x24"
    Paul and Doris Masa

155. BROWN MULE
    Oil 9"x11"
    Elizabeth Hulings

Typesetter—Set To Fit Inc.
Typeface—Goudy Oldstyle
Paper—Warren Cameo 60# cover stock

Photographs of paintings—
  Robert Nugent Photography
  Photographic Color Specialists
  Tincher Photography
  M A R C Photography
  The Arizona Bank
  Murray Getz Photography
  The Phoenix Art Museum
  Houts Studio
  Stephen Donelian Photography
  Pro Photo
  Ben Lasater
  Joe Mineau Photography